SONGS OLDER
THAN ANY
KNOWN
SINGER

SONGS OLDER THAN ANY KNOWN SINGER

Selected and New Poems
1974-2006

John Phillip Santos

Foreword by Dr. Arturo Madrid

San Antonio, Texas
2007

Songs Older Than Any Known Singer © 2007
by John Phillip Santos

Cover illustration of Aztec musicians from the *Codex Florentine.*

First Edition

ISBN-10: 0-916727-35-1
ISBN-13: 978-0-916727-35-2

Wings Press
627 E. Guenther
San Antonio, Texas 78210
Phone/fax: (210) 271-7805
On-line catalogue and retail ordering:
www.wingspress.com
Wings Press is distributed to the trade by
the Independent Publishers Group
www.ipgbook.com

This publication has been made possible with the assistance of a
grant from the City of San Antonio, Office of Cultural Affairs,
and the generosity of numerous individual donors.

Library of Congress cataloguing-in-publication data:

Santos, John Phillip.
  Songs older than any known singer : selected and new poems,
1974-2006 / John Phillip Santos ; foreword by Arturo Madrid.
-- 1st ed.
     p. cm.
  ISBN-13: 978-0-916727-35-2 (alk. paper)
  ISBN-10: 0-916727-35-1 (alk. paper)
  I. Title.
  PS3619.A597S66 2007
  811'.54--dc22
                                                    2007001499

CONTENTS

Screens

Albion Exile

Mexica World Radio

ACKNOWLEDGMENTS

These poems were sparked or touched by many, beginning with the great teachers and writers who first opened the world of poetry to me: Fran Everidge, Ernest Sandeen, John Matthias, Delores Frese, Thomas Jemielity, Dennis Horgan, and Michael Gearin-Tosh. It was my great blessing to grow up with poets always close around me, and they all left their marks on this work, especially Naomi Shihab Nye, Christy Walker, Denise Despres, Rich Landry, Gary Zebrun, Billy Hassell, Anne McClintock, Marcus Wood, Jessica Teich, Naomi Wolf, Deborah Esch, Sandra Cisneros and Carina Courtright. My beloved Frances Treviño, long-awaited *gran poeta de mi alma*, has brought me back to *la madre tierra* of ancient Tejas to share the path of poetry with two Chihuahuas and our ancestral host.

I am humbled by Arturo Madrid's eloquent foreword. Since returning to San Antonio, he and his wife Antonia Castañeda have been an inspiration to me in the challenge of bringing all of our deepest literary and cultural stirrings into the great agoras of South Texas and the world.

Many thanks to the American Academy in Berlin and Yaddo for giving me shelter during the seasons early in the new century when I began preparing and editing this volume. I was also assisted during that time in New York City by two young writers of great promise, Palmer Caldwell and Emily Lo, sent like angels from writing programs at Princeton and Columbia Univerisities. And, above all, *mil gracias* to *compañero* Bryce Milligan and his ever-inspiring Wings Press for daring to bring these lines into the light of day.

Some of these poems have appeared in *Cedar Rock, Notre Dame Review, The Texas Observer,* and *The San Antonio Express-News,* as well as in the anthologies *Salting the Ocean: 100 Poems by Young Poets, What Have You Lost?,* and *Is This Forever or What? Poems & Paintings from Texas,* edited by Naomi Shihab Nye and published by Greenwillow Press.

For Ernest Sandeen, 1908-1997, p.b.u.h.
Poet, Awakener of Poets

FOREWORD

I first read **John Phillip Santos'** poetry in its prose form. His family memoir, *Places Left Unfinished at the Time of Creation*, enthralled me. The telling was as compelling as the tale. I moved through *Places Left Unfinished* as if it were a sumptuous buffet, savoring the immediate aesthetic moment but all the while anticipating the following one. I paced myself, wanting not to miss a single nuance.

I have subsequently read John Phillip Santos the poet. The collection at hand, a sampling of his extensive poetic production, is no less a marvelous literary feast than *Places Left Unfinished*. Even the title, *Songs Older than any Known Singer*, is appealing. Its five sections mark different stages in his life as a poet, yet are all characterized by exquisite diction, compelling images, elegant turns of phrase, startling allusions, apt historical references, and always, engaging subjects.

One of Santos' abiding themes is loss, as experienced in leave-taking, in changing, in moving on, in forgetting, in aging, in passing. The earliest poems, found in the section "Walked-In Skin," reveal a sensibility that belies the poet's youth. "[W]e are travelers alone," he writes, "hoping that beyond/ our homes will be safe and whole…" ("For the Traveler," p. 3). Yet despite their often wistful quality, the poems contain affirming notes, as in the verse "I fell for love of the real" ("Untitled," p. 8).

Memory is a central motif throughout the collection, but in the section "Inevitable Fruits," remembrance informs almost every poem. In "The Same Face" Santos writes: "She would stare at me and say the same face/ My grandmother saying *la misma cara* the same face/ As grandfather's who died early on/ A face therefore that I never saw" (p. 22). What demarks John Phillip Santos' recalling is that ordinary acts, events, moments, and situations, invested with extraordinary meaning, are rendered in a low-key tone and deceptively casual diction. His moving elegy, "For a Death in the Family," is a case in point:

> Here follows a list which names some of those gone before:
> *Fermina Ferguson, the white one, a spoon in her coffee.*
> *The first of them, Francisco, dying young, perishing in water.*
> *Leandra Vela Lope, of a swollen tongue and the cardboard star,*
> *Rene Santos, who is among the war dead.* (p. 31)

In the section titled "Screens," the tone and diction are more elevated, the images more elaborately wrought, the themes developed at greater length. The poetic discourse is highly chiseled, as in a poem describing the topography of Appalachia: "Gneiss was there, meddled through with gentian/ and loose galena too, denser than any/ rubble" ("The November Screen," p. 42). Still and all, what prevails is the familiar, accessible, down-to-earth image and subject, as in:

> Cedars stooped to sweep near my dwelling.
> Rain clouds clustered there, then moved South.
> ("The Fredericksburg Screen," p. 53)

Santos' sojourn in England as a Rhodes Scholar marks the section titled "Albion Exile." The places, people, situations and events that inform his created world are different from those of his previous creations, as are his historical references. So too in part, by virtue of his cultural environment, is his poetic discourse: "We ate biryanis de camarón and borrego/ spiced anise and rock salt like fistfuls of posies/ sluicing it southward with silky porter" ("Oxford Punk," p. 85). Unchanged are his concerns, interests, sentiments, preoccupations.

In the final section, "Mexica World Radio," which features his most recent work, John Phillip returns to his *querencia*, to the space of his family and ancestors. But the poems reflect also his peripatetic life as a videographer, interpreting reality in a different medium and from a global perspective. Curiously he recaptures his earliest voice in some of them, but it is a more mature voice that observes the world around him: "Fireflies know this better than the rest of us:/ Only so much light in this universe" ("Saving Light," p. 120).

Reading is not, I learned early on, one uninterrupted aesthetic experience, but rather a set of discrete experiences, some occurring simultaneously, others seriatim, some cascading down, others seeping into one's consciousness. Never has that been more the case with me than when I read John Phillip Santos. I find myself immersed in his discourse. It insinuates itself gently into my sensibilities, heightens them, leaves them wanting more. There might not be anything new under the proverbial sun, but via his poetry I find myself contemplating life differently, sometimes poignantly, other times with amazement, still others with bemusement, but always in a more nuanced fashion.

– Arturo Madrid
Murchison Distinguished Professor of the Humanities
Trinity University
January, 2007

A NOTE TO THE BENEVOLENT READER

This is a book that was never meant to exist. Not long after I started writing and publishing poems in the 1970s, I began to write to the legendary poet, Laura (Riding) Jackson. I was a teenager in San Antonio, Texas; she had an address in Wabasso, Florida, that I found in a writer's directory in the local public library.

I sent my first letter to her in appreciation of her poetry from the 1920s and '30s; dense, abstract, philosophical and obliquely beautiful work. I had written to other poets – William Stafford, Denise Levertov, David Ignatow, among many others – every now and then receiving back mildly encouraging words about setting out on the unlikely path of becoming a poet late in the 20th century.

Mrs. Schuyler Jackson (as she signed hers letters then) wrote back, chastising me (at some length) for not knowing that not only had she repudiated the work I had extolled, she had repudiated poetry itself – in 1938. After living in the literary capitals of the West, since then she had dwelled on an orange farm in rural Florida, working on a book that she said would correct all of her errors and establish a new literary paradigm.

While she averred that her poetry was of the highest order possible in that art, it nonetheless failed as a means to communicate human truths. Poetry was a hopeless machine of artifice and effects, she insisted, betraying the deeper mission of the human: To seek and express truth. As she would often repeat through our years-long correspondence, it was not just that her poetry failed, "poetry itself fails." In her counsel, to pursue poetry was a folly.

I would only learn much later how many writers Laura had affected. Perhaps like me, they were moved by her fever for truth, her ardent belief that our words mean something, and that we must always seek the most direct means to communicate the truths of our knowledge and experience – what Laura would come to call "The Telling." For me, that became journalism, documentary television, and non-fiction prose. I stopped publishing poems, but I was always writing them, hidden away in paper scraps, notebooks and journals, stashed out of sight in drawers and files, embedded in the deep astronomy of a nebula of hard drives in old computers.

I learned of Laura (Riding) Jackson's death in 1991. Late in her life, she had written, "I propose that you seek in yourselves remembrance of the Before, and write what you find, and believe your words." I returned to re-read her letters and I began to think again about what it means to put your poetry out into the world. Encouraged mainly by my longtime poetic conspirator Naomi Shihab Nye, I warily began to publish poems again, in magazines, journals and anthologies.

This book that was never meant to be gathers gleanings from my ongoing unintended chronicle of a secret life in poetry. For better or worse, I've left everything as it was at its creation, the shifting regimes of stanzas, capitalizations, punctuation, the unseen manifestoes holding it all in place. At the very least, as Laura's life implicitly acknowledged, poetry must be allowed to fail on its own terms.

It has been said that life begins in poetry, and ends in prose. But poetry remains.

– John Phillip Santos
San Antonio de Béjar
December 31, 2006

WALKED-IN SKIN

For the Traveler

my sisters and quiet brothers who weep
are as homeless as I; in our dreams
we see our houses burn and clothes fade
into a penumbra of smoke. like sleepwalkers

in a desert under moonlight we face the night
without gentle crescent to lay us down in. oh sister
in this evening of sand have I not touched you?
your fine limbs leaning like bridges into me.

but soon, will I remember your eyes?
as tender leaves dipped in gold we keep a brilliant figure
in visits to only the caves within us.

we are travelers alone; hoping that beyond
our homes will be safe and whole, a large tone
vibrating slowly between the poles of the world.

Portolani

Before dawn, the wives would gather at the docks
holding high the candles that burned with the smell of wine.
Their prayers were sung in heavy breath that sank
to the sandaled feet in a mist, the color of babies' veins.

The men woke to this sound of morning dirge, rhythmic
from the shadows of masts and the sails, flapping now in first light.
They left their shacks with bread or souvenirs of dirt, but the captain
lingered in a cot with the din of a sparrow's bones snapping in his
          dog's mouth.

After the ships had left, the women started like blind ones home
hugging the walls and sensing the walk damp on their feet from the
          morning tears.

One who waited, watching the bodies grow smaller on the horizon
crossed herself with the candle; beneath her feet,
saltwater slapping the dock's pale wood.

The Word

She had a name for those nights
when she would not get to sleep.
The laughter of crickets, the hard darkness.
Inside her chest, her heart would jerk
and whir, like a projector flashing
cameos of undressed men against
the milky temper of her skin.
For these hours there was a name,
a word so guttural it pulled at her,
but she would sometimes forget it.
Morning was another veil to wear
netted on her face, wafting in the beach breeze.
And always she wanted to scatter
and be sown like colonies of seeds,
to cast her jewelry away from her
into the tight weave of the reed roots
by the shore. Walking back to the cottage
she would imagine the many shining parts
of her, filtering like anchor-shaped spores
into the regiments of sharp grass. And how fine
the sand can feel falling up against
the feet. There was a title for the awesome times
and she told it to me once.
The name was long and foreign as the continents,
and I see her there in bed
awake and disturbed by the way the lands
rise and fall like tide, and there
floating above her would be this word,
this name which could comfort her
with its dull vowels and tenor consonants
that sounded like a fisherman walking home,
his hooks ringing in the wind.

Remembering the Poem

Impatient and hot, I heard your knocking distant
from inside a dream I was having
about lovers killing themselves with long, thin pins.
That day you were here to show me a poem.

My friend, your body has wasted,
all its pigments and edges drawn into the garments
that commit your figure with starch;
your vest was perched on your shoulders and its buttons
stared, the gaze of an animal nesting in your chest.
I gave you the day-old butt of uncle's cigarette
and a sheet of paper. You slowly balanced like a scale
and began to type. The poem came from memory,
standing over the typewriter like a piano, you would forget
the time, and curse. It was the percussion of the keys
and your simple furies that started me laughing.

Your signature was large and affluent
but when you penned the date you asked
the spelling of Wednesday. It is a hard word to spell,
its shapes jagged, lost in the middle of the week.
You left with all the urgency of your small beard,
another soldier off to do battle with a mystic.

The poem was about death and a lady
whose kiss brought a premonition of your end.
I was reading when the small letters began to shine
and spin, all the punctuation marks giving off a fine smoke
the form of feathers. My hands held the paper tightly
as they might have the first picture I saw of a dinosaur.

Elegy *(Never Delivered)*

She was massive
in her huge furs
and coffee-stained smiles,
her words were stone.
But she liked parades
and she bit into them
like inevitable fruits.

Untitled

In sleep, my waking mind
clangs like a zither.
Hillbilly noise of the ordinary
filters down, surrounds
my skiff, adrift in the still water.

But there was little gravity
inside the great arboretum.
So I climbed, past
many tiers of galleries
up the tree of the world.

No one watched, not even
the birds hidden behind leaves!
From each limb hung
all our illusions of desire:
palaces, undulating bodies,

machines spinning wildly
on steel lines. To look down
on the world was to change it.
Map lines, light as fingerprints
emanated in waves across the oceans.

Jungles to deserts, then cities
rising out of deep gorges.
My dead grandmother's words
first became a mountain range,
translated into birds flying off
never to return.

All of our lives lingered in the air.

I fell for love of the real.

Long Ghazal

for Cynthia

That her father perished in a flash of light, or
her own body, seen once against a floor of ferns.

That the land of Nebraska waves to the brim
for a pocket of sand and a hill's diameter.

That he found her sex, and cupped it gently.
In the kitchen, on a bandanna: six green beans.

That every assortment is slowly revealed to her
in fish hooks, in glass, in folded paper.

That he left the note on a porch in Oklahoma;
she discovered an old door floating on the river.

That mercury will bead up on any fabric
and the shadows of trees on the sheer, chalk bluff.

That she could return to stroll the avenue,
the task being to guess the order of the signs.

That the decorations themselves are the story,
her reflection in the bell of a saxophone.

That her mother worries for her daily,
the milk bottles empty, arranged on the step.

That she laughs before the cheap, warped mirrors
along the shore where she will find the shell.

Acquiring the Hand

I was acquiring the hand when
worms could plead me to spare the hook
or I'd flop the nets scap-free into the ocean.

Jesse built his boat and I steered it out
everyone watching, steered it out past the salty fog.
I took the wheel and we plummeted.

It was at eleven, a kíkapu rocked the canoe
reached over and grabbed out a fish
a gar, gasping and making flap.

But when I was acquiring the hand
there were creeks everywhere! Flood-swollen
swum through with fish, like a land of plenty.

I'd visit them, trace their muddy profiles.
Each day I could try my luck
could rig the pole, tying line and hook.

Where would they be biting?
What would be the bait to use?
To stand there waiting, my cork on the water.

Those who had the hand kept their secret
the lights going out at the end of the pier
and then the sea itself subsiding.

Radios broadcast the chronicles of fish.
So I listened for what had been caught
how big, and where each fin met its fate.

To have the hand meant everyone would listen.
The stories would be told now.
And the hand was a road from the mountains to the coast.

And the hand was the first day of all fish.
To step your way onto the ancient breaking pier
was to have the hand, and it was sometimes risky.

So I called down the bank, "fish on line!"
and the bamboo quivered at last, while
my hands learned the pull of bones themselves.

Someone said that it was the hand.
How these beasts run silently under water!
How the colorless fish shines against the sand!

Expedition

Through the opening door, a wasp's
descent and flight, awash in the
spreading light. There's a table

in the mirror, where waxy bananas
shimmer alone, becoming crescents
that glow against an absent moon.

Platter of fish bones. Tempera
measured in a glass. How for months
we culled a desideratum of love

from those moments when we'd tumble
headfirst, farther into our skins.
Moor hens and street cats

mixed in with our paragraphs on the
peaceable kingdom. A world
assembled from these tuileries

of words, a pageant of declensions
drawing us out to the open fields.
There was a sky we saw, all made

from the multitude of our longings:
Arcturus and Pollux, Alpha Orionis.
And then like Raleigh desperately

bound for Guayana, we floated out
onto a vast ocean of pauses
and inflections, deeper than we

could ever hope to plumb. 'Til now,
or this flicker of falling instants,
where unprepared, we're taken in,

towards these melons appearing in the
kitchen; a door that swings out
to daylight, that's daylight, with cicadas.

The Fact Which is Everything

Everything is the year where the body grows thinner
It remembers its own bones, retreats to their keen.
The body imagines itself deaf and forgetful
But is only losing its way –
And there is a way in the world.

You come to the body in an enormous car.
It is years since you've driven
And the avenue is narrow, so, embarrassed
You tumble down the street, soundlessly.

In the silence it is everything that happens at once.
Your watch stops and you try to honk at people
To get the attention of anybody
Weeping at bus stops when suddenly the horn fails!
The temperature plummets!
You think: *I am growing old.*

In that common hour it will do your little body good
To remember noise, when any sound will do.
Anything but silence, on either side of talking
There is silence only, the racketless car, the body
As you think: *Only so much to be said.*

Later the body is skin and bone, the body
Of the father, and of the son leaning over you
Listening for your heart, amazed at your ribs –
How tightly they are woven! How much like hands
Fluted and clasped, saluting upwards!
Small facts about the world are spiraling
Quietly inside of you.

So when it comes to hands across your face
Looking for breath, you will want to remember the fact
Which is everything: where you parked the car,
The time, the temperature, the look on your own face,
As you hear a voice almost in another room,
It says: *He breathes.*

Zarzamora Street

This morning I woke to crow-kaw
and the mumbling blues of a black
woman visiting on my street.
I remembered the moon, last night,
above Amaya's grocery trembling,
that bitch Elena Abdo, who sells
Mexican curious from her booth
'til midnight, yelling:

                        cuuuuuuriooos
baaaaaratooos
And the roses in Señor Bailey's
garden were losing their petals
one by one.

Recite: *All that we count best
in our lives has a shape, and will
remain itself 'til we die
and ourselves are no longer ourselves.*

INEVITABLE FRUITS

Sauza Talk

1.

Our confidence is in the neck
of that guitar, the swooping belly
John, of its varnished torso.

Let's begin with this world:

Where the custom of the cat *Blackstrap*
includes two meals taken daily,
and his memory
which inspires him through the hedges
street-ward again, to take
good knocks there upon the head,
and he returns wet

like a beggar's clothes,
jumping from patio to window sill
where his paw will tap
two times to the bell string,
for the ringing we'll hear
across the house.

2.

Bless us we say for what
we shall now receive. Again bless
these kitchen cups & breakfast table,
the door by which we entered,
and this bottle come ye new
from the ancient land

when I was bearing into creation
the elixir of agave!
A sap so sweet
squeezed through in 1942.

This, the tray Naomi left out
and another seven limes sliced
half-wise.

Certainly we know a tornado
from a train passing, if we must
even, to check again and see
is the roaring wind there, or not?

3.

We need not evacuate. *Was*
a train we saw, heading north.

Not a cyclone, not a *terremoto*
wrecking the habitats of possums,
not the flood and not
the great storm which comes,
which comes –
not even the blue armies
stomping in the streets,
or the neighborhood boys
with airplane engines in their cars,
not murder, not death itself.

But a train, probably bound for Chicago
and probably the black engineer
who keeps her running
is asleep at the helm
and dreaming.

4.

Fill the cup fillup & let us drink
a dram once or twice about the house
& leave where we began!

Drink we to George Coleman, who is Bongo Joe
and has a proficient song on the oil drum.
And to the star of Palestine, Naomi
singer of our very same song.
Drink to Frank García of ninety years.
His was the dump-truck that has moved worlds.
To the mate of all roads, the dog Jeremiah,
he enjoys his feet to be rubbed any way.
And to the Brother Batts the crazy and insane,
that he has followed his map back to New Orleans.

And let us discuss now
the garments of great men!
And let us diagram also
the labors of bees!

The Same Face

She would stare at me and say   the same face
My grandmother saying *la cara misma*   the same face
As grandfather's   who died early on
A face therefore   that I never saw

I've seen faces   I can match back
to someone I know
Somebody I met four months ago   hitchhiking
In Pontiac, Indiana   or   a man seated by his groceries
At a bus stop in Albuquerque
Same face   *someone I could say hello to*

My grandfather had a moustache   dark like shade
the Earth lays its shadow over the moon

In a photograph he is strolling Houston Street
package in his hand   I see El Tenampa bar
A man selling papers   The Buddhists ask
What was the look of your face before you were born
Probably same as now I answer

I ask myself   Could my face have another name
Would it then be the same   I don't know

Cara misma she would say to everyone
same as father's father   also named Juan

Maybe once all faces were the same
How much Nani Abdo   looks like
Florence Delao!   that lady on the street
might as well be Aunt Fermina   last name: Ferguson

A face is a place   with geography   history
Whatever name is given it's given a day only
America Africa   the giant shelf called *China*
Names spelled with dust   the place remains the same

Grandfather arrived home   package in hand
brushed his moustache with a toothbrush of tin

My lip is bare   but my smile is the moon
crescent   upside-down   lighting up my cheeks

Standing against the wall at El Tenampa bar
I take the scene in   try to place the faces
In her kitchen grandmother stares at me
says the word   *curioso*
measures some bleach into a chipped blue cup

August

Outside the month is changing   August
will be the truest month and will be the month
Not like July   of deep-singing animal sympathy
but of the simple story
that is   your life

And you wait for August   so he pitches his tent from your door
But did you expect he would
bear mirrors   history   paragraphs in our common past
that you might come to believe something about yourself
a detail that was never important?

For here I am a man kissing the lobe of her ear
Here I am a waif filling his pail at the well
I lean back   and I am a donkey kicking into the air
Here I am the famous one whose feet are adorned

You are revealed in August by the riddles you've told
A fog has rolled in so we mail all our letters
At last our signatures tremble like dust onto the stones of this world!

"You have not been honest"   August says
(You are reminded over and over for 31 days)
What has four legs   then two legs   then three
There is no world other than this one
Your face makes no promises   now
what are you

My answer is that the trees all look the same
until I come to myself   make out the circles I've walked
There is someone waiting for me   at the other end of the forest

So it begins here in August   I'm passing into another quarter
It is the never-expected harvest   it was
the evaporation   the terrible sound of examples falling together
You pull the venetian blinds to pass the hours alone
You're finally deceived!   You know what's real!
We had made no plans for the utter surprise of it
August is a long month   it even carries us into the cold
the world says: what are you   who are you

This time you're alone   you have a small fire on the stove
and are warming yourself some beans
The calendar rings   August 10   You remember
People telling you   One day you'll wake up and then
You'll know   You'll be sorry   You'll think better

There is the sound behind me   behind   coming closer
A great white bull reaches me   lifts me between his horns
People are waving along the streets of Pamplona
alone and exalting   into the air   I'm thrown
into the air and ready to fall
up against the ground for the very first time

Wetback

I.

At midnight swimming the river   walking North
Flowing East   the Rio Grande   and we rest at its bank
hear the water mumble toward the Gulf

Walking North in the dark the lights of Reynosa dissolve
into the twelve-song hike to Edinburg
Corrido de Texas   Volver, Volver one song
I sing seven times   I depend on every word
I sing as loud as I can
In the bushes   across the plain   there are
many wetbacks   I see their t-shirts glow
all night my songs twirl up   tell them: I'm here

The distance between Mexico and Oklahoma
is enough   to remember everything done or said
How I did it   my shoes will wear out   my feet complain

From Edinburg one night's walk   a man named García
his ranch with a two-story house   I eat
sleep   have a dream about crossing the border
into sand   behind me
my house is howling its only song   endlessly
over and over   the future is the past   the world
leans North   do anything but rest   always return
make any guesses   about all things   along the way

II.

Blessed is the man who has work   and can do it
for his days here will seem right   will rise like smoke

into the opening body of what he does   It is
a man's work that makes him right with the world
I am a man who says   this matters somewhere
a place were all we do is not   chaff on the wind

But who is blessed   Do you love what you do
To work   I am here to work   that explains everything
You show me the way   I'll make the world every day
Are you satisfied   Do you want to cross the border with me

No use   I say   In this world the ones who   want to
Cannot   those who can meantimes   will not
I knew a man   could've carved a feather
on the knot of a tree   could've carved
spoons   ladles   bowls or plates
but he'd say to me   I take the knife and I'm afraid to use it
I'll scar the wood or rough the grain   the bowls
on my spoons are always lopsided and too shallow
His wife would yell at him and cry   and one day his son killed him

I am walking for the day to work and be happy
like my friend Peñitas   Blessed is him
for he tunes pianos   and sings on weekends to widows
and he castrates pigs   and he fixes leaks
and he drives any car   and he repairs all kinds of springs
and it is good in these times to know many things
every penny he saves   to marry his sweet *Polaca*

III.

Let me show you a photograph   of my father   working
in Cotulla Texas   1919   his name was Blas
turnips in his hands   two in one   see   three
in the other   his brothers: Santos   Emiliano   Flores
are counting turnips   look here in the corner   a man is stacking
them into boxes   I don't know why Papa is holding five

Seven times he swam across   mailed us money back to Villa Union
He'd return   in the winter   sometimes   with gifts
cinnamon   two bolts of colored cloth   a bag of chewing wax
He taught me the river   where to cross it
by wading in the shallows   through the passages of deep
you must swim across   in the night   like a buffalo

El mojado verdadero   he said   will swim the river so many times
his tattoos will wash away   he will come over the hill heading North
the water says to itself   There comes Blas again!

So my mother would pin the photograph to her apron
take it everywhere she went   and our house was made of mud
so when it rained leaves would blow against it   and stick
Afterwards I'd walk outside to peel them off the wall   my father
sent a letter   saying   God bless you
There are pipes to fit in Medina   pipes to fit in Medina

Piedras Negras

Seventeen days in Mexico comes down to coins
in my pocket. Pesos, three nickels
I find a dime in my wallet.
Up to a mile away, beggars hear the clink of coins
and I'm ringing mine openly.
They will come dressed in their parents' clothes
and uncle's hat; they'll look at the lines of my palms
when they take my lode of coins.
Alone at the edge of the country
all my souvenirs, the memory of having been somewhere
mingle and settle like a dust
across the back of my shoulders.
Every time the wind rises up
I lose a bit of what's happened.
Consider my cargo; a clay flute, bought for eighty pesos,
the wool blanket, a pauper's bargain at two hundred,
the day I traded six ball-point pens for a pair of sandals.
And there were beggars everywhere
Asking for money, a vegetable for their morsel stews
or just money. Some sat on church steps
giving out pictures of saints in return for tiny change.
They appeared in my dreams as deer, donkeys, and goats
that I would feed all day and night.
Before you leave a place behind you,
give everything to the beggars,
come away weightless, take your shoes off at the door.
Today the beggars do not arrive.
across the street, a boy in a wolf-mask
yells that he is going to eat me. Some women walk by
with bundles of wet alfalfa on their backs.
Looking for beggars in Mexico, nothing is as big
as a fifty-cent piece, ordinary people the size
of Emiliano Zapata's eyes
going white in all the old photographs.

For a Death in the Family

Some of them went as anyone might: with time,
and others by water, a joke in the heart, a machine.
Some of them may have dug fingers in tomato beds
until the very day came, abandoning the ripe herb fruit.
There are the diaries leaving off without premonition.
A man takes a card with the name he'll chip into stone.

We buried Grandmother in Laredo, then ate pinto beans
with mountain chile and coriander past the border into Mexico.
Along the streets, we saw automobiles stop, the poor
removed their hats, and flushed their dogs from our route.
Behind the church, I hired a lady to sing the old songs
and she wailed and moaned at the edge of the open box.

And some line up statues across the shrubs of a garden
the wealthy war dead with moustaches and muskets of stone,
of marble, or bronze, and chiseled in spite of what is remembered.
Uncle Santos, the fanatic, is no longer among men.
He has expired in his Buick on the way to preach in Pleasanton.
A grey morning, the car idles against a cedar post.

Grandfather, a foundry worker, swam out into the empty water,
man-faced and unbending, in exile in this country
who told the foreman people are not meant to work.
In an act of contrition, he'd taken his sons into the ground,
tunnels where box cars glided by, full of ore.
Men with blackened faces against walls of sulphur and iron.

But that his young son should find him there, cradled
on a dark wave. That alone, he might have to collect
a man and see for himself all mercy, all tranquility,
the floating body. This could not be the truth.
He remains there, beside the magnolia tree
and there is no grief, a paragraph in the paper list details.

Some of them finally called it a dumb show, Bill the fiddler
just before he went, could hear nothing but rattling tin
and the mid-air collision of insects echoing through his halls
as if inside the walls of a waxed palace. Disappearance
was another scheme for those who went elsewhere without notice.
We bear their commemoration, benedictions for the sake of them.

Here follows a list which names some of those gone before:
    Fermina Ferguson, the white one, a spoon in her coffee.
    The first of them, Francisco, dying young, perishing in water.
    Leandra Vela López, of a swollen tongue and the cardboard star.
    Rene Santos, who is among the war dead.
    Afflicted in the bones, Grandmother Margarita was lost in sleep.
    A friend, Felipe, beneath the Nueces, brief and deep enough.
    Juan José who also perished in water, weary and of his own.
    And cousin Lydia again by water, for the good sake of sleep.
    The attempt was made to save him, Leonides was lost in bed.
    Then the lawyer García, whose blood became water in his veins.
    And remember Cristobal, who took his truck into clear air.

You, primo, will go by means of a surprise regarding breath.
Blank-eyed without time. Your wife exhibits against the porch
your open lung, flimsy as old fabric. Through it you can see
the massive sycamore with white bark reflecting the sun,
and maybe it is the cure, maybe after all, it ends
in the catalogue of seeds there, ready to drift onto the final world.

Geology

Along the table edge
          midway through
an urgent hour
the crease in the map
          runs skew across a shaded aquifer.
Her songs   her songs
dwindling from another room.

Following a broken parallel
          the words:
coniferous   *limestone*
          Llano Basin
where we found a fossil of flowers
          blanched in dry Silurian mud.

This region's process
          water passing through porous rock.
The acid of the soil
blades of alkali
disjecta membra of ancient life
seeping through these
          where a cavern hollows out
where oil runs through fields
          fields of rock
of limestone   many miles down.

Her shadow appears on the blinds.
She is undressed on the patio
          moving toward the gladioli
as she pauses in the simmering heat.

If she should call me again
       I'd show her damsin quartz veins
       struck in Blanco's chalky cliffs
or walk her past Encino gorge
       out beyond the garnet mine.
Plains of limestone
       vast beneath us
veteran windmills that always spin
draw out endless seams
       of dark cool air.

With My Old Friend

We ate in the city, "this city I love,"
she said. Driving barrio streets
I couldn't convince her that too much
of what's not good accumulates in a city –
dust, sickness of body and mind,
needless deaths by knives and guns.
       In her favorite legend, streets become countries,
       places only themselves, yet vivid, mysterious.
Vagrants wore sunglasses in bleached January
light. Their destitute breath reeked to me
like medicinal tea, but she went among them
talking and laughing in their pidgin drawl.
At another table, Italian pensioners spoke less,
nodding off into the television's mid-day news.
       "Let me call them out," I said, "into the streets.
       they'll march as an army, their burdens left behind."
Her arms were thinner than I remembered,
the muscles of her throat moving lean and quick.
When she saw sadness, I saw infamy
and life in her city was always lives of women
and men as all times before in all places.
In the streetside clamor, I embraced my old friend.

Texas

Here, the oak claims it true dominion.
Here, the cactus deserves a purple blossom.
I saw the falling light of the stars,
the shells of ancient bees, for the first time,
here.   I'm leaving again . . . who knows how long?

SCREENS

Colophon for a First Book

I can say that I am arrived here
by navigation, having known when to enter
the temple and when to consider it
from one or two miles away. Often I have seen
a flock of gray ptarmigans pass over towards the city
and there known that should I follow them
in town a precious fortune awaits me, fruit
bartered cheap by a blind vendor or my brother
in the marketplace crowd with his new wife!
But today I am unhappy and confused.
My wife has been gone three days
north to pray at the bones of her mother.
My son climbs through trees all day long.
It is evening now, and not long ago
an enormous parrot glided past the door
into my kitchen and perches there still
staring over towards me, spreading out his wings
as if his feathers were the light numerals of my fear.
His body is yellow and green, his head
ignited with red. The long beak yawns open.
I see the dry, compact craw.
What do you mean bird? Why come
to my home? If only I were a seaman,
those who live by sign and measure;
the sailors olive-skinned, lean, and distant
watch the sky, its tongue of color
check the gales tugging at the hems of the sails.
They are trying to return, to show everyone
you can pioneer to the edge of things
then set course back, but you must read your way.
I am lost and can no longer read.
This parrot has chosen my house,
I have offered him grapes and he has refused them.

He is only his own steel glare and great orange claws.
Do you bring news of my wife?
Has my son fallen from a sycamore and broken his bones?
The parrot waits quiet like a tabernacle of secrets.
What is the whole world but a quiet
where we guess at the meanings, wait for graces
and assess the losses? I am confused.
Outside, pearl-colored beetles maneuver in the esparto grass;
with me here, the parrot sits, an elegant riddle.
And then amidst all of this, just now
the mammoth grace of a white moth
as it curved out of the darkness
to tap my chin and pass away again!

The Angus Martyr

Fifty years past, he had watched a cow drown itself
rather than be herded into a pasture bordered by rusty fences.
A black Angus pledged herself to the ancient mud
of the brown Rio Grande while the boy yelled
"come back" from far away across the dry land.
The cow had come from Mexico where there were no
fences and the thing went down into water preferring
the regions without wire. As a man, the boy
would remember often that sad Angus martyr,
he would rise up out of his sleep with the suspicion
that miles away cows were lowing at the moon in pain,
he would fall back only to dream of cows,
how nightly they broke through fences like a part of him
with their stupid bodies and enormous heads.
He would have a son born with a long, furry tail
like a cow's, and together they would build fences
because fences are the sufferings that must be built.
After a day of stretching barbed wire across cedar
the boy that became the man would drink black coffee
while his son out in the pasture would call
to the cows to come lick at the salt blocks,
calling with a deep animal sound stirring in his lungs.
The fences went out like lines that never finish
and every night some beast would try that tension
letting the fences ring, post to post across the land.
And every night the man would tell his son
about the tail he had been born with, its gentle fur
when they cut it off just after the child's birth,
and about the great black head of that Angus bobbing up
out of the Rio Grande, black hide glistening with mud.

The November Screen:
Turkey Farms Under Aurora Borealis

for Denise

Patience or faith, says the weatherman.
Miles out, we walked down by pines
farther out to a pond, leaf-riven, that seemed green or dark brown all that day.
What craned our way was a logger's footpath and LaBombard's slot-fallen wall.
Thick moss was heaped scarlet as Mercurochrome
on ragged banks of gray stone.
Appalachia's ruins shifted beneath,
all rock and dust scratched in jags down the hill.
Gneiss was there, meddled through with gentian
and loose galena too, denser than any
rubble. Quiet and unnoticeable
we stared out from a hill's basement.
In other times, we might've come to stay
forever, face to face, dumb as Quakers,
like animals in a family zodiac.
But no books could say who left that old land
behind, without mementos of their lives.
We saw evidence: Whose cabin, abandoned?
Their names mixed in with vegetables and lost.
When night arched the lowland, maples darkened
with birch and hollow elms through the meadows.
West, or lower, to the South, a vaulting
deer fell closer when someone's gun
rattled, spraying buckshot through the bushes.
A patience, known from railroads of Ohio,
widens and widens, making rings that will
inscribe cities and smoke, patterns of streets,
dusk-light over Lebanon, New Hampshire:
and finally a bee, an ear's queer shape,
or both mingled, on pieces of broken glass.
Then, to find us loving in that forest
beyond the lamenting noise, or tears and wrecks,

saying here's this body, here's a small virtue.
Other sounds leaned out from the darkened walls.
Far-off warbling, the wracking call, out from
the pipe of a turkey's gullet, answered
then by another farther out, a hen's
noise, jerking and stopped, becoming fluid.
Later, almost a song, or a turkey
displayed in flight over blank, wasted fields.
Dropping at last and falling to quiet.
Didn't you hear it? There, over the wind
or the cars, hissing down some graveled road?
Three men emerged outside a patched-up hut.
They saw blue, wavering fires
and fishing barges on the lake. Pink,
the skies went mauve, to purple, until
snakes found shelters and shed greaseless skins.

———————

This world is all decoration, as in
sidalcea delphinipholia's
ten petals. *Viola canadensis*
late-blooming around a pond's muddy lip.
Someone gazes on this feminine land;
sees ridges and escarpments, horseshoe bends
in a river's way, or mended acreage
throughout Pennsylvania.
These are lines as we found them, these scars
are water-marks of the ancient cataclysms.
Now, lighter, an umbra of gold waxes
before nightfall, there on the horizon,
unexplainable and too brief for sight.
Plots of planted land were laid out
semaphore-style, with asparagus spears
and berry patches, dilapidated

threshers where barley once was
cleaned. There was nothing here, he said to us.
No walls, no wheels, no blessed cross,
nothing named and nothing seen.
We brought it all and settled by the lake.
But ploughshares fall to shovels, and shovels
are left buried in the ground. Time is short
before Lebanon goes back to grassland
and grassland is little better than scrub.
We took a place amidst the numerals.
If there was color there, or geology,
or even commoner things like beauty
and memory, we took a place amidst
their workings. Tens and sevens, and sevens
and tens, that were the quantities
of the place: were miles, were names of settlers,
were canoes turned up, were lights through the flume,
and the ways we fell closer to the world.
Words dangled above those things which remained.
They were savage and uncomfortable
sons. Vermont dwindled, then Franconia expired,
leaving the clear impress of a thistle
in the plaster that will be coveted
and hidden. To tell these decorations...
A nation is a cipher, ash on age.
Mexico, I thought, beneath
its rugged antiquity
might be this way, stripped of all poverty
and its history of calamity,
left fallow for centuries, discovered
again, abundant then, in future time.
We'd braid one world between us: quartz cliffs
in New England, and the dales of highland Chiapas.

Like El Dorado, a golden foil background
on a foreign scene. To redeem
the falls, of Jefferson in Virginia
and Lewis at Council Bluffs. The two of us
waiting in the notch, found a dark way up,
some ferret's path between two shelves of earth.
Sediment, Aztecan mural,
or a pageant of the years, was silent
alongside us. Battlements of limestone
and a flourish then, of mica. What's there?
Whose death? Champaign, in a silver pirogue
disappears through the fog of the salty
St. Lawrence. Those were good years for Cod.
A city grew, cinquefoil and populous.
Then skirmishes are shown, flotsam of war.
Sandwort, *arenaria squarosa,*
a time when a farmer on these borders
ploughing hills under curving steel
shall find heroic bones, or vegetable
shapes, if not some desiccated relic,
or deeper down, a pagan alphabet.
Instead of dirt, speckled ribbons of decay.
A scabrous history is lurking there
of this perishing domain,
of old words, as massive as dinosaurs.
Or ancient machinery,
and the ruins of beans, still in their pods.
What does not change is imaginary.
Our works, this world, our failure to outlast:
How the procession of the wild quickens
always toward you. And Hsu-Yu
threw his hand into the waterfall.
He washed his ears, his tired eyes,
and washed his mouth and anus.
He'd met the black bull and wrestled with him,
horned and shimmering, walking
on the high road to Edo.

He washed away the sweat of the fierce beast
there, at that waterfall, and stood alone,
amidst cypresses and grouses and gold.
Turkeys looked up toward our stopping noise.
On a hill above the town
we might've made these pictures persistent,
to begin with Iroquois
drawing turkeys on cliffsides,
or the Bedfords, later, hunting turkey.
And their colored feathers in a cascade
pasted ascending on your bedroom wall.
I saw no mist on that night.
Thoughts of Mexico. Color: Japanese.

———————◆◈◈◆◈———————

It was a wedding, seen through a window.
Not a blue-grey dove or a fishing skiff
with its oars at rest, not a rare truth shared.
Only something happening in some way.
History bites like nails into hardwood,
yet what is remembered will tell you little
of the figures seen that day
whether of the men who built
these walls, or a man-shaped rock
that scowls down at us, waiting by the road.
Move forward in a blindness, until something
calls you back. Furniture, or blank spaces.
Nothing's there, nothing that tells.
The smell of fish is a softer thing, mud
mixes in with rotting hornpout, and oil,
then washes to the color of the sky.
Suspicious, meandering scent, settling
through the thicket, the air heavy,
and heavier on the peat of August's

leaves. Color, in the pitch-sky
was later, but not in glorious streams:
seven long veils of dyed gauze,
splayed up against the Northwest,
and almost invisible.
We danced like apple-pickers
on the last day of season,
would've sworn that things were drawing closer.
Homely names, out from this whirling plenum.
That something true might be shown,
in the way we've seen Saint Francis, kneeling,
penetrated with brass beams
of merciful divine light.
Aurora Borealis, dumpling smells,
when the wanting absence of sound precedes
catastrophe, a drunken partridge that slams
against the living room glass.
Come closer, come closer. Contrive to rouse
in us some knowing prospect
of love, and all virtues
of attraction. Where's my sleeping lover?
I've crooked behind some kettle reed. I've crawled
like a crab against her decorated
fence. My love is rising now,
in her dazzling house as bruckle as air,
and she strokes her hair, with a comb of bone,
though her eyes are crulled with sleep.
Imagine the scene again.
On top of a hill, in my bed at dawn,
as witnesses beneath the Northern Lights,
taken backward into a curving smoke.

———•◦◉◦•———

Birches shivering. And pasted with fog.
Or is that a grainy pall, lingering
after Sunday's bonfire, and everyone's
heaps of burning autumn leaves?
Calf hooves quietly bit into the turf.
Forever, this crisscross static of stones
gathered and fitted, without mortar, for
a wall that will tumble, and thereafter
remain. All goldenrod's like a fire,
like a legion of bright-haired girls, tracing
the hill's diameter.
Milkweed seeds spun out on the wind, tangling,
pushing through the thorn and briar patches
to shuttle past rocky ground.
But I remember it beyond what's real,
maybe seeing things now we couldn't then.
There was a river. It's called Maskoma.
To the people of the place
it is with them always, in the winter
bearing them towards summer,
and in the summer, it shall
cleanse them and surround their bodies with light.
At one time, it's said, animals touched there,
like children;
the owl with the weasel, ducks
muzzled close with skunks. And this wild was then
blacker, calm, ploughed. In your uncle's garden:
A bush of cranberries, the crippled thrush.
These, the figures they made in the mud, many
years ago, of turkeys and beavers, mice
and pelicans. Ravens, hawks, moles, and gulls.
Yet, those trees remained for us the dark sign,
along with the light draining from the dale.
Candles burned at the end of the highway,
while the graves contained their dead. They had pressed
their bodies to this ground, and felt it move
beneath them. From it they took
asparagus and summer corn, gardens

of dwarf convulvus. And that
was their time, their pain. Now something
had changed in the valley's rasp.
Change is the diet on which all subsist.
Created changeable, it's change at last
that comes like jagged music.
Concordia discors, a little faith,
he says, a little hope to get you through.
I'll try to show you a field of fifteen
Irises, fulgurant, and in full bloom,
beneath an eight-plank bridge. There, the dipping
petals, speckled with a flirting gold.

And there was a crown of land
that seemed to cling around us.
Down the hillside, from the canopied pens
where turkeys lagged in gaggles, their brackish
calls were no sound of mourning.
Their doom was sold, and just a week away.
Still, above them those lights would coruscate
on their diminishing spindles, striking
the outline of some single tree standing
at the crest on the far peak.
But to try to see it, to make the first
mistake, then soon we're scavenging for more.
What's a world made of, but a
phalanx of tumbling words? Begin from there
and see back, to a single thing at most:
an acorn's cap, or a slug on some stone,
and that will be the strangeness that bristles
all around us. As when I saw you first,
naked and close, both of us trembling
that such intimacy as these bodies

could seem so foreign in quivering light
against linen. Or coming then to you,
how it was a kind of absence falling
from between us, invisible quiet,
that corona of stillness where we met,
and as if from far away,
moved back towards the world, and our talking
of many things of the world. Then again
there's a scene...of herons on a backdrop
of gold. Where the last one comes,
a hornet nest's hanging from purple blooms.
Korin made his gold paintings on leaves of
bamboo, with honeysuckle
and flies and ladies of the noble courts.
Then he'd toss them to the stream,
rocking in the spick-torrent, lingering.
Or some, floating down, to where the soldiers
built their fires on the water.
We made an imaginary heaven
that rolled and flew with the scrabble of our
living. How little we will see, whether
Meriwether Lewis, or old Cho-Mei
at Toyama, in this mutable world,
and we in it, blank, under our houses.
Twelve catkins found in a dry marsh's bed!
Your teeth then, your tongue, slipping on my ear!
As we went further, along the open
ridge, the river's murmur ahead of us
became duller, then resumed.
Flocks of birds, in trees, couched the falling night.

Starting Over

It was the only road, old and crooked. It went South.
You noticed it was a road you'd taken many times before.
There were the reminders, the things left behind.
A straw hat with the shape of Mexico embroidered on it, your wife,
an old suitcase, the shoes your grandfather took off
before he went into the bushes to take a piss and never came back.
All of them waited roadside looking small in the sun.
You drove faster than usual.
Along the way you passed those natives who sell iguanas,
magpies and weasels. They yelled for you to stop
but you went by them laughing and honking
until you saw your backseat full of foxes and rats,
in your rear-view mirror, the desperate stare of an enormous hawk.
You threw back tacos, chewing gum, and a jar of marmalade.
That was the day the beasts ate well.
The day you lost your way. The road eased
from rock into dirt and you told the animals how much fun
to move so fast and not to recognize one thing!
In the village of Atontonilco you stopped to ask directions.
A hag with a moustache sold you a blanket
and with her cigarette traced out the roads to take.
It was easy, you wouldn't miss it.
The road ended at a river where a child
Told you that a week before the bridge had collapsed
and all the bricks turned into geese floating downstream.
The little zoo cooed in the backseat.
Already weeks into your journey, you were lost again
parked on a street in the town named Bernal.
On the sidewalk, a drunk soldier fondled his old trumpet
playing a messy tune and forgetting it.
Through the backseat window he saw the bellies
of sleeping rats, the coifed face of a little fox.
Your maps were covered with hawk dung.

The soldier returned the trumpet to his lips
and your gears whirred as you decided to start over,
The rats burrowing into the springs of the seat
and the smell of fried corn from a vendor's stand
rolling toward you down the narrow street.

The Fredericksburg Screen

Veni Redemptor, but not in our time,
Christus Resurgens, quite out of this world.
'Ave' we cry; the echoes are returned.
Amor Carnalis is our dwelling-place.

– Geoffrey Hill, *Tenebrae*

Cedars stooped to sweep near my dwelling.
Rain clouds clustered there, then moved South.
In this way, the wind kept things going.
Two winds headed gulfward, dust and rubbish
with them, arching the trees back to themselves,
leaving them hunched down or kneeled at the shore.
There, the mighty trunks lean over, pointing
out, on the expanding face of the Gulf.
Then live oaks lined up like a field of priests.
Animals stirred there, leaping from the branches.
Aphids, bores, and caterpillars made meals
on the bark. Wind looked out in all quarters.
At the cliffs past Fusco's, echoes sputtered
and disappeared at last in the canyon.
On a donkey, I made my way against the wall
arriving then at the bottom. The rubble
of twenty years was there – kitchenette chairs,
lumber of old houses, something gold in a lump of shit.
Something tumbled into a pile of rusty tin.
Leaves were falling from above, over the bluffs
down to me, on the floor, where old newspapers
celebrated the centennial of this town's founding.
Banners had flown out over the streets of Fredericksburg,
new flowers were scattered through the cemetery,
a live deer was chained to a parking meter,
a day illuminated by the past, and the mayor

in the omni-congregational church retold
his story of the settlement. The floods had come,
then returned after the sickness, and then the fire,
and I found old Fenmore, leading his mule
back from town. He was almost Mexican
when Mexicans were not allowed to stay.
And many would die, they said, drowning in a creek
or falling asleep in front of an advancing train.
That day we rode to the empty stables
with his pictures of the Virgin of Guadalupe.
Fenmore remembered the tornado that took his wife.
He'd broken horses for a living, so his bones were bent.

It began for me earlier with the cattle, when
they would await us in their pastures by the road
to Fredericksburg: The Santa Gertrudis, the Brahma,
Herefords, and Angus – they were the great breed,
stupid and enormous, masticating their elegant cud
with a steady twine of drool swooping from their lips.
I gave a black cow the holy name *Asunción*.
Then I found a cow dead, struck by lightning.
Of my talking to cows there is not much to be said,
only that we could line up alongside a fence
and sing low *moooo*-cow, and then they'd come,
to stare, or stick their bobbing heads over the wire.
What preserved them was their utter lack of imagination.
There was no need to go anywhere, the rain
came upon them and left their hides refreshed, the sun
and moon exchanged quarters, the open pastures
bristled with new grass. That was the mercy of the world.
And we'd drop the blocks of salt from the first field
out all the way to the cow's pond, chopped cactus
or burned yucca for fodder when the pasture was low.

Then they fought among themselves, the bite marks
of a bull or flesh grazed on the fence's barbs.
In the night, from the shack, we heard horns lock,
their great lungs abounded, thundering around us.
Adolf died, left his cattle without a father, so we kept
the place until Merrill could take it over himself,
and that summer was a hot one, the tongues hung down
from the heavy jaws, the muddle of manure turned
quickly into dust, what finally would remain, we supposed,
would remain. And we expected only that the Pedernales
could continue flowing and something in the ground
would suggest that the pines might throw their cones,
for in this way things could be kept going.
But Merrill let the thing fall, fences fell, wind
fell hard onto the house and slammed the shutter,
and hooves-up, the cows perished in the empty pastures.
We dragged their carcasses from the back of the old truck,
In that land on end, in our tumbled down world.

ALBION EXILE

Factories at Southampton

In America, I suppose, It was to botch
memories of the Gulf, especially how
we heard all night the Drum's missive
croaking beneath the hull. The pills

we took slid down like clam shells.
Awake past tide-fall, mining the shoals
of bream by the petroleum tower, my mind
was already slooping elsewhere.

At which latitude will you remain,
unsayable, quill, soporific, when traces
of what's happened sway first, then
disappear? These incandescent towers

are a legend to another country.
Some things reminiscence cannot change.
The manipulation of memory is a bitch
to the heart. Desires we cull

from a clutter of fears, and we
breathe it in the salt air for hours.
If I float off from my past, gradually,
grabbing at briny crab traps, or nets

taut as a ganglia, I would want to meddle
in Christen's anatomy again, to let her face fall
from the night we mapped a rainy alley
in ancient Veracruz. In slower time

it could involve a theory on the skeletons
of fish, an argument of liberty, and at last
a freeing of the catch. I might never call
in this port where smelters heckled from

their mills and eddies of oil spun in the slime.
It would be America, probably, with my knife
again under the crab's eye, to be lost at sea,
towing in, our radio warm as a voice calls back.

Letter from England

for Ernie

Rain again, the sun dial in the garden is useless.
For weeks Atlantic squalls have rolled over
this town in dense grey swathes. Weathermen say
a wall of warm air is stalled over Russia
and the Communists are hoarding our summer light.

When time passes here, it's bacon frying in water,
a quarter-stick of incense lit on the mantle,
or we talk, briefly, about umbrellas and elections.
News of the world infiltrates these rooms in papers,
through the wireless, or as foreign scenes
blurred and wavy on steamy glass in the TV screen.

He wrote, "Forget about those wars in Persia.
Concentrate on peace talks between armies
in your head." But, spooning sugar into coffee
with a knife, that seems a false difference.
How we install our territory of necessary lies
and mark it off jagged as a mountain border
from all these outward things,
the inaugurals, laws, and decapitations.
They say heavy weather's beached like a freighter
on top of Brighton, they say every damn
struggle implicates us a thousand ways.

Two Easters back, Oxford re-staged a 17th century
battle here known as the Bloody Day at Marston hill.
I woke that morning to the sound of cannon
blasts rattling my toothbrush in its glass.

The battleground was on an easy bus line
and a cloud of gunpowder smoke seethed along
the streets. The illusion was complete.
When churches let out, all the families
lined up watching from the decorated barriers.

Out the attic window I saw platoons clash
and separate solemnly, dragging behind them
black carts of antique war equipment.
They were making a war for the hell of it,
following some old story they'd been told.

Red banners floated over the winners like thoughts
in a newspaper cartoon. "The toll was staggering,"
a voice announced on the loudspeaker,
"yet the King's forces have held their ground."
Providentially, armistice had come before tea-time.

Now the Isis is flooded. No boats going out.
Inside for days, Marcus and I concoct the perfect
tetrazzini, reading Marx, who wrote to his father,
"I hit upon seeking the Idea in the real itself."
In 1837 there must still have been a difference,
when slow trains trailed steam on rocks outside Berlin.
I dream tightropes stretched in a big top,
waking dizzy in the library, falling backwards.
Not to worry Marcus says. It's just *quid pro quo*
as things happen, these days, at this latitude.

The Early Call

In the room where I slept, daylight
washed through Ingrid's curtains,
false speech of remembered talks.

At Quercy, this light comes bald
against the painted face of a bluff.
Horses run there, hunters lap toward
the appaloosa print of a hand.

My heart was made macadam since
the grating. If misery loved company then,
it was in movies, like Edward G. Robinson,
dying, in "The Woman in the Window."

He'd said, "Imagine your body
as a woman's without penis
but breasts, a lithe, feline neck."
I encumbered on my morning erection.

When light spread over Banbury,
over the hills, we saw the laxity
of their shape. I drew in my body's
remorse, a space between the legs

As a woman's naked, a painting
in the Dutch style, my children among
the living at the quay. Crinoline shag
lay all around the morning room.

Following these thoughts, I made them
also. Though happiness will elude,
she said, "This I must do, I must."
For hours, steam whistled out from

The underground mains, and Keats
who lived near here, would start his day
in this way, aimless, afraid,
shoulders churning in feminine light.

Adams's Well

Whether in hatred, our own blood
thrilled with greed for the old sufferings,
     or even deeper,
something left undisclosed,
     as if decorated wrestlers
grappled there, plumed, underground:

> *someone called up a law against*
> *the moving world, in a sentence,*
> *a stretch of music on a mandocello,*
> *in rhetoric's secret power . . .*
> *while we looked down and saw*
> *the Queen's swans in a patch of reeds.*

There will be no pictures of me.
I that was in health and gladness
and knew some moments
     in the light;
     only to be troubled now,
parsed between two griefs, one infirmity.
Self-portrait of Samuel Palmer
picture of Louis Zukofsky,
and both, seeming embalmed, spooky.
     Where in other places they dance,
     here they are like to die.

> *Beautiful calamity . . . a figure cast*
> *and hammered out in the magnificent*
> *forge-house of language, serpentine,*
> *concatenated, a bridge between*
> *this world and itself: Panama*
> *linking South America with North.*

Everything filters finally through this
ancient well, dug twenty feet deep
  filled with rubble and roots, clutter of years.
Whether water, or juice of rotting Winesaps,
or the drain of vegetable lavings,
   here'll be this old canal
   washing through a rocky alphabet.

Field Day

Fokkers rattled over Frognal, buzzing the heath
in an aerial tribute to WWI. They forgot tea that day
under the unmistakable growl of war-planes.
She saw raid columns, ladies with buckets, flashlights,
scrambling to cover drop flares when Sheffield was battered.

Today the queens do not walk the park.
Today a flaming MiG crashed in native territory:
in our exclusive footage, see the pilot safely
parachute earthwards.

And flying machines shivered and banked
shaking their Remingtons as never before,
made a gauntlet to smash armies of the air.

"The beauty of the trenches . . .," one man hissed,
"The beauty!
when we'd sleep under the splendor of the blasts,
breathing steamy yellow gas."
His haw shook his dentures bad.

Up the hill, residents kept a zoo
with exotic animals from all over the globe.
The man there gave his calling card:
                    EMERITUS KILLER, M.P.
and spoke calmly of the "gift of electro-shock"
raising an open hand over London's skyline,
toasting "the natural pre-eminence of one race."

That was their *paz mundial.* Applause resounded
as biplanes meshed and showered overhead.
Out of such things, she thought, will come another remorse.

They tuned in as soldiers took Beaufort castle.
Through television, where history swung pendulum-style
over the world, they encountered the hostile legions.
The territories were marked out with banners.
They entered their own thoughts reluctantly
and consoled themselves for battle.

Testimony

To a soldier or a priest or the sea,
      and for the sake of a single thing,
I say, that it shall remain,
      our lives, some history, an old map.
Women are beautiful, and Wars,
      their flesh, the exquisite machinery:
We've seen from here a shining
      that comes at night, pylons
against a burning sky. And sex
      almost like a scent of gas
Or anemone, goes out upon the wings
      Of swallows and swifts and daws.
There was a parade first, a promenade
      Of Belgians and pipers, grinning
crawlers, marsupials, and ape-faced
      children, sleepy in the sunlight.
Mournful, they went along that way,
      Trailing banners and smoke,
There came then shooting, pistols
      rapped hammers somewhere
in the dumbstruck train. Animals
      fell there, and humans fell.
The Tyrant's planes banned the air,
his eerie fabulous garrisons
darkened the chalky bluffs.
      Others lived in a pleasing time.
Indescribable foliage rilled
      In loops and spirals by the gate.
There was mica, iron, and diamonds
      jack-eyed through the dust:
The bodies of their women were shaped
      perfectly, in the taut, thin ankles,
and the curve of the bending calves
      womb, breasts, and face,

portrayed in paintings on the walls,
        and their speech showed as curls
or commas yawning from open mouths,
        rising, twisted, musical.
Years by days were graven
        into pitch-dark stone,
until the myriads dispersed
to the North, to the South-East
And some who had been savage
left gardens floating on a lake.
We've traveled out to unmarked borders,
        slept in the hulls of abandoned
cars. Mexicans in crowds
        wandered out into the streets, singing,
calling, powers in the wilderness,
        back-looking, forgetful
of all things. What I saw
        there was this World,
broke-backed, still pleading,
        as the sediment eased, by colored lines,
finally into place. And coronas
        appeared around the poor,
when we scrambled out for shelter,
        amidst oaks and bunkers and dusk.

On Rectory Road

Where one house was gone
its outline stayed, years after
embossed in a rusty shadow
on our building next door.

Down the street, mullahs moved in.
Their past was in phonograph records
calling the devoted to prayer
with nose songs like braided tin.

We learned to call broccoli *calabrese*
to satisfy the Pakistani grocer.
His back was bent like a question mark,
left that way by coolie work on Aswan dam.

Formerly Pembroke Street, the sign said.
A photograph of former times, where
a heavy-coated woman stood blankly
in the door of a cottage, now absent.

Asleep next to you, I dreamed two women
swaying with me in our Connecticut bed
making love as if you'd become two
or I had come to you as woman and man.

We entered this speech of unseen lives
through the simplified time
of our street calendar. We slept
on each other, waking to car noise.

Questions kept us devout.
Over breakfast, as if nothing were true
we argued DEMOCRACY or MEMORY,
drinking coffee with Irish and Greeks.

In the mirror, out the window,
gables of the convent blocked
our view of the old city spires.
From your bath, you'd ask for a towel.

I would bring you anything.
Each step toward you trails a story
of parades, fireworks, how our street
is little, while history is vast.

Scalding water leaves your skin pink.
When the house flies in open sky,
out on the prow of that placeless city,
only our bodies fix on points of the compass.

London New Year

Mud rakers and tramps looked up
from beneath the bridge, beyond the gulls;
they stopped a moment to see us coming.
     A barge bound for Henley
had been loaded that morning
with iron scraps and sulphur . . .
and a yellow mist
     blew out behind it
          all the way down.

They shuttle through old shells
and find aluminum
and prophylactics,
     the driftwood they burn in alleys,
or a herring, lacking air,
blushing on the grey bank.
I say to her now:
     cast away your shoes
         cast them down.

A canyon was filled with water
in Texas, the hole
at Sutton Hoo with dirt.
     Implements of older life are retrieved
in knives shaped like trees,
golden vials full of sand:
and Dan dove down –
     he found roads there,
         empty, watery towns.

The government of London dissolves
with dusk. Relics of Cotulla
can be seen on the river! 1843 . . .
     only fifty-eight men

by then, in Oxford, farming
the land between the factories;
or Laredo, that New Year's day,
      when the bodies of forty
           young Mexicans are found.

Legions of tramps stumbled back
along the levee walls
while gentle trains passed and fell.
We kept no souvenir, no map
or diary of how the year passed.
Only darkness as we crossed,
and darkness with seventeen skiffs,
      floating towards Greenwich,
          braziers glowing on their polished decks.

Epistle on History

to Adam Ashforth, at Finstock

No dialogue should include a tiddly-wink mood,
my fever beneath this tea-colored light, or the way
the clouds rattled and blew today, when you took
your spokes and chains and dawdled back for Oxford,
but all things coming apart, Compadre: the world's
a ragged rickshaw, not a ruby on a turtle's back.
The fire which men once worshiped is crept into
every chimney, burning rubble, or newspapers, or time.
That dandelion, a fair plant, and tall; see
the deceptive way it's rearranged with the day's passing?
A flowering first, then a kind of sphere made of knobs?
What moves the thing, if not will? Chemistry,
perhaps, memory without intellect,
or maybe some latitude that's scrawled right in the dirt.
Mendel knew nothing of peas or plants like these.
The wind caterwauls across the hedge roots
and plucks the seeds like the last hairs
from old Dolly's pate. Thus creation
first kisses the forehead of sure annihilation,
the way Spenser saw it in his *Preludium*
to Book Five of *The Faerie Queene,*
or Donne, in his *Anniversaries,* the gloomy chant:
Shee, shee is dead; shee's dead: when thou knowst this,
Thou knowst haw wan a Ghost this our world is. . . .
and then again, Shiva makes his toothy shuffle
on the fried pall of what we've loved in this world.
Yet it's too delicious to be true, isn't it?
The theme of decline that's not without purpose?
It's fit for embroidery, or a plodding Sabbath sermon.
What's real is this blank space, that rises in our bread
or belches up from the gut. It's the mirror trick
we all have to play by, dreaming or awake.

I saw your Mother pick a primrose, and braid it
with her past. What fell away was the darkness
like dew rilling from the stem, but this
at best is delusion, and the very best we can know.
And then I will imagine a pleiad of Negroes,
black mussel-eaters, Hottentots,
and how they welcomed the flags of the Dutchmen,
smiling on some beach in sixteen twenty-three.
Or the Aztecs, my own, and their limbs spangled
with feathers. Cortes saw power in their strangeness.
He made them feed on rocks and reeds and scree.
This is the frequency of the vanquished, a kind of death
that loses its spindle as it gets farther from
some sympathy for itself. So the Mexicans
worship horses now, and like Arabs, the black men
wander the world. You wander out now Adam,
and bevel some idea of this shifting plenum
into iron, glass, limestone, or tin.
Your friend will count again the lights you've
seen before, across the hill, at Charlbury.

His Only Regret

Of course, he'll defer to someone's
riddle cue, or, the fatalist,
dismiss it as scrap in time's clutter.
And though less than savage, it's true

that his candor exceeds his guilt,
not to exclude one detail
of the parable, to render it
entire, in all its smutty splendor.

How ticklish this slipping constancy,
and 'the gentle,' jostling amidst
our sullen privacies. Cartoon-like,
such popping-out of the eyes,

that marimba swelling of the heart.
In the daguerreotype's marrow
he detects the seediness of their grins,
beaming undaunted and callous.

Called upon in the holy fray
whether as dilettante or dapper
guerrilla left to scramble
in the jungle fusillade,

he openly surveys the moving
parts, suspicious always, straddled
in mid-air, taking the license,
reclining in her pungent charms.

Then left to follow, crawling
placid, de rigeur, "in these deathly
times, our world emitting the fumes
of banal fetor, kin to shit,

so hopelessly derelict. . . ."
Yet come to this, could he make
new life from the scuttle that's at hand?
Blank video screens, shrapnel flying
in the political domain;
a virtual Frankenstein of scattered
viscera, including Nixon, again,
bloodthirsty for the coming war.

A Manichean gloom stirring in the East:
The breasts of Elizabeth Tudor
on the body of Che, pictured
dead, Lazarus-like, in La Paz.

Old Film

The pioneers were con-men,
Dime and nickel operators.
Hawking absinthe money off gimmicks
and hand-trick stage bluffs.
In the dark, their voodoo
flourished. It was an old world
of mirrors, ropes, thin brass hoops.

"Voilà," they'd incant
over the heads of the mesmerized
audience of *cognoscenti*. Gloved hands
revealed the absent dove nightly
for a quarter-day's wage.

When the lanterns came
to *Salon Indien* in 1895,
It was "German Dragoons
Leaping the Hurdles," they saw,
screaming and dodging
to let them pass.

On the screen, when time
ran backwards, it jerked
the breath out of them.
They gave the ovation grandiose
to their pirates of the real.

Their world was more real
then than now. Lenses fell open
on empires of daylight
to find workers leaving factories,
bottle-washers over troughs,
armies waving in tropic light.

Pancho Villa rode on Monterrey
with the cameras of Hollywood
alongside him, saber drawn,
tilting his horse to their eyes.
It was a time of famous moustaches.

They saw the world in scenes
separated like buttons on a factory
line. Flights over Everest
fading to Natives at Victoria Falls,
then Sacco & Vanzetti on trial.
Some mysteries remained: The Queen
eating oysters and Africa's deepest mines.

Maps of Asia could be re-drawn
with a stylus. The face of the Czar
carried to the country in satchels.
Private life became slow and transparent.
In letters home, cinema light was magic
to conceal. It was a final geography
of cities and men, a new secret life
in machines, gaslight on beige linen.

Untitled

There was never any reason for worry.
In that time of running into the streets
like haunted gangsters, the demons passed by
one by one in evenings lit by a trance.

Hands that came through windows
were friendly, in need of apples or money
and every door opened to reveal
another desperate traveler anxious for rest.

They would laugh at what other people knew,
the facts of love, their maps of the truth,
and stories of two minds becoming lazy,
losing contact like drifting rafts on a lake.

It was never less than a fire made of words
and touch, holding hands in bed,
they felt their bodies pass like a torch
through wreaths of memories and pledges.

She had called them turning days,
when he would turn into her, seeing
clouds become cliffs, becoming mirrors
that showed trees dropping late October leaves.

What they knew was left for other people
to say, the man with the nine dogs,
the queens who sell jewelry on the streets:
Embrace now and confess the invisible world.

Struggle Speeches I *(Sonnets of Dissent)*

Forget the fathers of this land, their lives
ideas, their documents. Now we must begin
the glorious thousand years of tyranny!

Savage their names, the patriarchs, founders
republicans, slave masters, amphibians
filthy progenitors of antiquated lies!

Our politicians and bureaucrats mirror
the ooze, sleaze, and cupidity at large –
show us larceny in hearts, minds, bodies
in our very fingers. Long live our leaders!

Freedom, equality, fraternity are the shams
of a bygone hapless age. When we sleep
our dreams shall proliferate like television.
We'll wake to declare peace in our veteran world.

The Waiting

What the people will linger for:
jobs, food, and news from the front.
Some mysterious men are thieves!
As junkies, they loiter with roped mutts,
peddling old newspapers and cantaloupes.

Out of need, cops will keep them waiting
at the corner of the street where I live.

Waiting for the animal to stop that yacking.
Police dogs blankly frisked him before
the tap of the club, the advice of the judge,
when waiting is against the law.
And a grin as the noose tightens on his neck.

And the people never know when the Mayor sleeps.
The workers keep him awake with snores
like jet engines, so he sleeps during the day.
Executives and generals have no time to wait.
Their business allows no sleep at all.

If they could sleep forever, the people
would abandon unemployment lines.
Their rents would go unpaid,
their phone lines clipped, left in darkness
dreaming half-frozen in broken beds,
'til bosses wake them from the dead.
Then it's off to wait again!

Sometimes in winter, a rotten leaf's outline
remains scorched on the sidewalks
where they walk. Where pockets and purses
burn their hands in ice for hours:
the bank clock, busses behind schedule.

The Book of Woman's Laughter

By the radiator, where four sweaters are laid
to dry, an idea of beauty wants to dwindle, darken,
lose its momentary eminence in October light.
The idea is in these, our simple disinhabited shapes,
in sleeves pressed flat akimbo, necklines encircling nothing
as if it were always noon. Falling light late Tuesday
allows and diminishes the accord, his parenthesis within,
her great love inciting some desire to know its object.
When I talk as if love and hate were the same, I mean
we hardly know what we think, pausing side by side,
until in sleep, we can dream with the innocence of beggars.
You have met me again there, in a passage full of ladies
or with the señores, smoking in the gutted bell-tower.
My heart belongs to the most sorrowful of bitches
and when she sees you, she will be full of hatred.
Page to page, we make out illustrations in a daily primer
settling differences on authority of this fundamental book.

Oxford Punk

We ate biryanis de camarón and borrego
spiced anise and rock salt like fistfuls of posies
sluicing it southward with silky porter
boasting hopeful new tattoos under x-rays
until they glowed and gradually faded
amidst gorging ourselves wondrous
in an ancient Sunday vindaloo parlor
on the Hindu furlong of old Cowley Road
in our pennywise broke-down city of learning
another frittering dusk in a darkening yuga.
One name had gone off to Brighton, she wrote
"to meditate on a being in my belly,"
one stepped barefoot on a fishhook
one had hit the road with a blighter
she said was once back-up bassist
from the original Teardrop Explodes.
We, the inscribed, we who were left behind
had since forgotten the original question.
First came the lightning of the pleroma?
First fierce winds across mute earth?
Or was it always the word, the word, the word?
One by one, holding breath, each of the forsook
dove for scarce gold coins into a river of Beaujolais.
Hey, somebody start a fight now, he said
no easy task in a warren of wet, empty streets
fling a bicycle as far into the night as you can.
Over the wall, into a garden full of topiary sky
or better, through a living room window
where the last progeny of empire
would be sleeping through reruns of Benny Hill.

MEXICA WORLD RADIO

From the Brown Book

I.

Weighted with bricks, bound with wire
and walking that way until stars hung low
where the river met a river, turning west.
We went far enough to change the sky
and still there was more. Never enough
to make up for the time already lost.
Never enough to atone for walked-in skin.

Rain falls sweet this time of year.
The sow's ear, the belly of the kid, or
grizzled neck of grandmotherly pachyderm.
Rest now, at the bottom of a river.
drop down to where alluvial silt rushes
out toward the ocean, past bridge
and buildings and indelible footprints.

II.

A blunder of sweetness in the muezzin's
call to prayer. Trembling in an instant
that opens out almost to a laugh
and then flashing awe or fear that
returns him to that voice of all time,
when dawn is visible behind the neon mist.

Here, we will treat of the beginning.

III.

The amaryllis reveals its blooms slowly
while we wait days over half-hidden
fronds that gather sustenance for the bud.

Amaryllis, hawk, ice shelf, espuma –
the sepia haze that envelops the city

that we might divest ourselves
of all that has remained unsaid,
all that remains buried
and unnamed.

I will walk through your speech
breathing in the fever and age
you mean to make on me.

IV.

Let's not try too hard
to talk the way we always have.

Our heads look separate ways
as we move around in the steam
of city streets.

Vengeance will be hers.

For what was done before,
someone must pay.

It was in the month of champions
just at the edge of a bad feeling
there were flower stores
where blue lights basted orchids
in a frozen window.

V.

You breathed your life, like a diver through a snorkel.
You saw swimming lights far overhead
marking out the x's where people had visions
lived by coins or stars, understood the perversions
ordinary men are capable of in this world.

My words must've come in clear on the radio.
You could walk to the lake and float a tube
just to break up the day. In the back of your car
a book lay open on the page where you finished.

VI.

Deborah captures her words as easily
as she turns a page. Maybe, she says,
it's a new world; so completely new
those words don't mean anything
to anybody anywhere. My dreams
had been talking about it for weeks.

VII.

Everything there was as it had been.
The grease on the walls reeked of
ghost bacon and made the place
feel warm and familiar. Grillwork
filtered gold city light onto what
had been bookshelves the way he'd seen it.
If they had become pantries then,
or counters for showing souvenirs
from a trip to California,
it was somehow part of the truth,
following the roll of things
out of what the world was then.

VIII.

The time passes slowly in morning light
as I rub her back with the dark moist air
of German autumn. In sleep her body twitches,
strung between my arms and the ether of dream.
Where we slept had been roofless,
neatly lifted off by a bomb before
the days when the occupation took
the house, and a rotund colonel
took sun in a chair on the garden terrace.
The prowling soldiers used pipes for target practice
and stuck their chewing gum any place
they could stick a finger.

IX.

Earliest hurricane ever. Doing cobra
pose in the rusty afternoon light. She comes
on land like a lady when I count 20.
The flowers of many kinds, long-stemmed
in a vase. Past the duck-blind kitchen.
Ate that for the first time
and will never regret.

The physique remains,
as weather.

X.

Wake up the mission from terraces
where tables were left scattered with candles
and cups of wine. Out in the desert
the Indians had been playing snooker again,
taking aim in dangerous honey light.

If it was now the sleep of middle summer,
cutting like beveled obsidian across
the arc of the sky, then only the bells
would wake them. Only the deep underwater
ringing of those broken taboo machines.

1964 Sonnet

His early fear was losing those he loved
or their loss of him. At the window
in December tremendous were the cars
of other people, splashing light in gutters
as they passed. Somewhere in that darkening
town, the best was always abandoned,
in Southern Pacific railroad depot's
rusting Apache, arrow-drawn, atop the dome,
or Gus Garcia, in tequila soak, wrapped
with newspapers beneath a market bench.

Toward court house square, as tribes
in tarnished Ramblers, driven to the fountain
where pennies were the dead, they threw them
by handfuls. And colored were the waters.

From the Spanish

for Ludovic B. López

I.

Off the shoals where armadas were anchored,
       off glinting flecks
of brass and malachite, off annals and parchments
where a reverend destiny was inscribed;
off their Pyrenees, off the people's brackish past.
         One dream coiling through another dream,
               into that obscure jungle . . . these promenades
                   of infantry mute on the soggy land.
For weeks, the heavens would rain sickly blood.
There no lacy ovation brayed, no luminous eye
to crack some new Toledo into this volcanic
world. Then, in grave, rolling numbers
their brooding god declined his yellow brow
down to them. When at last their words expanded,
they meshed outward, to forge a net
that wafted down, covering this world:
                 Fuimos, Vimos la Matronaza
                 Sentada alli en la Sombra
                 de la Higuera Chumba . . .
Bernal Díaz de Castillo gazed on maize;
he saw a vast plaza crazed with music-like speech.
        From the Hill of the Spindle Whorl,
             with pumas and obsidian staves,
                 a flurry of consonants flew up
and blackened there, above them, in a cloud.
Full of disbelief, with a touch of sleep
the new language ambled out, inspecting the thorny floor . . .

II.

Anno Domine. 1767, on the twelfth of August, in the pueblo
known as Villa Camargo, Tamaulipas; it is duly attested to that Don
Fernando de Palacio, sent by the eminent Virrey de Nueva Espana,
and in noble duty a mantener las tierras Mejicanas del Rey, did
gratefully cede *dos fajas de tierra,* two plots of the
territory, to the scribe José Gómez Vela who had greatly pleased his
eminence in the service of canvassing the population of the land. In
1783 the granted lands were purchased by Señores Bartolome
García and Miguel Chapa, who in turn vendieron las granjas in
1818 to Don Antonio López Bermudez, un anciano de nuestra san-
gre, and grandfather to Cecilio López de la Garza. It was Cecilio
who along with his wife and four sons, Evaristo, Biviano, Pedro, and
Quilino, first crossed the Rio Grande at Anno Domine. Anno
Domine. Alleluia. They carried with them the deeds to these lands
of Nueva España, which to this day are known as *Paso del Teo Adame*
and *Cerrito de los Canales.*

III.

When the carpenters arrived, they carved their capriccios
onto juniper and ironwork. They forged new cities
from the shaking of the air. Throughout the land
          a miraculous order was emerging,
where the Indians ground their scaly cochineal,
where colonels smashed the dirt into fiery doubloons,
hammered the moon to cast a dome.
At Guanajuato, blessed rats crawled
on avenidas of gold, laughing monks
left streets that elapsed into Atlantic calm.
              And in the square, sucking on yucca and tamarind,
                    the Holy Fray Pedro de Gante solemnly
                          baptizing thousands in his saliva . . .

Tassels adorned the ripening corn!
Endless arrays of fraying Catalonian silks!
Sent to us in their boats, dissolving in the banners,
       how little our language is truly our own, yet how
       it takes us deeper, past the world:
curving up and around like a vivid snake,
cascading with the peals from imaginary bells.

A Naked Man Jumps Off Harlem
Works and Days

I.

We are in Heaven. From here, Falls Road,
Gates of Harlem, festive ghettos in the Philippines
can't be far away. We know
another world – sleepwalking in a bombed city,
trains bombed with Persian writing,
bombed maps, doors and underground passages,
buildings bursting great flames or gutted.

We exhausted every breaking skank funhouse
in those terrifying plots we read under siege.
Nachos and figs would make us faint, necks turned
on greasy spindles, legs working like switchblades.

And then we saw, *Are we bad or what???*
And thought, yeah, bad, insidious, the worst ever.
Poke '83 and *Etee One* were everywhere,
but the people were nameless, feet in brown gauze,
smoking butts, coats pulled up to their heads.

Streets in Heaven are convoluted and friendly
like the meat of the brain. Banners are strung
between buildings, proclaiming *La Verdadera
Avenida de las Americas!* In our own heads
we make or break laws about sleeping, death, fat toast,
and sex. We study maps of the USA in Russian.

From Heaven, we see lives spinning in watches
dangling back and forth on a fob.

Taking laundry to wash in mail bags from countries
around the world, talk is always of living,
the trace of days and nights we still follow,
how some flirted with fascism in Indiana
and others found language in the arms of lovers.

We learn essential lessons of what to forget,
what to lose forever. Great ones are here:
Frida Kahlo, Blake, Neruda and Artaud.
They see the numberless poor
as lines in the golden landscape, stones in scoured
valleys, beige lines of sediment upon the scene for miles.

Churchill and Stalin divvy the whole packet up
with a pencil on the back of an envelope.

We gamble and lose heavily at the cockfights,
asking, "Is this Heaven? Is this Heaven?"

II.

Barry was strictly a runner, a corner man on Amsterdam
with two kids that kept him in the city fifteen years.
Before that, his old man bought the farm in Jersey,
left Barry to scour up bus fare.

His office was the sidewalk at St. John the Divine,
"where the pigs see me glowing in the dark, like a saint,"
he said, "and when they catch me, we kiss like lovers."

When there's a shakedown in east downtown
his trade moves up foggy subway tunnels below Harlem.
On the street, bankers and junkies are edgy, full of fear
for the great she-elephant, she who must be obeyed.

III.

Weeks later, a second winter would begin on the island.
When his bare feet left the lumpy roof tar,
toes curled and pointed, head pulled back,
arms bowed back behind him and still,
he was already breathing new lungs in Heaven,
thinking of a red needle in scorched grass,
still clogged with sugary strychnine and scag,
with a body beside it, blue, curled up, tranquil.

In Harlem, he thought, hot shots explode common as
bottle rockets ricocheting at Chinese New Year.
He would fall for the cameras like an Acapulco diver,
thrown naked from his mother's fiery arms into a perfect notch
when waves swell against miles of jagged cliffs.

Naked and bent up in the street, the caption reads
"After war, no one wants to stay in uniform."

Photographers are just grateful to have caught the scene,
expecting a jumper or two only, in their entire career.

They get shots that will sell anywhere like a Raphael.

IV.

The year he was Commissar of the feria,
the town painted him a wonderful book
made of playing cards, pigs in his favorite colors
gold and gray.

He used his only eye to find compadres in the crowd,
handing out Havana puros like wooden nickels.

In Heaven we are better friends
than when he made me smoke a stogie

at the edge of Canyon Lake, saying
the lungs are two rivers that lead to the head.

From the teak liquor cabinet he would extract
a stony corroded bottle of Cognac Napoleon, 1871,
burning our mouths with capfuls of icy orange.

"Bottled for the King of the World!," he'd say.
Another lousy dictator, I thought.

We share Sulema's chicken soup, eating avocados
from a tree thousands of years old.
We marvel at Nueva Rosita's chimney stack, tallest
in all Latin America, sitting silently
in the shivering afternoon heat.

V.

Numberless phone calls. The thick glass of the coffee table
fractures first, then shatters. Tofu, marinating hours
begins to smell like hemp.

I miss our weekends in New Haven,
the trees split by ice, the interminable questions
about pizza and culture, the conspiracy theories,
and watching Breshnev's funeral with old Black Panthers.

Pulled down the shutters, dowel and all.

It is four in the morning in Heaven, and we move on to *noise*
and how it is we know it when we hear it.

In Heaven, they call this time *the divine crack,*
meaning the end of world, meaning the revolution inside the carnival.

Sumpúl

I.

Morning of oregano smells, smoldering ash.
Drizzle through a roof
packed with palm, mud, and straw.

Las Aradas on the Sumpúl.

A ply-wood bed where Sibrian snores.
The children are awake. Sibrian sleeps.
He snores waves of oregano mist
from out of the jungle.

They would say:
The motive was clear. They built
low walls along the far bank
of the Sumpúl and we could see
their horrid shirts working.

Dawn light, grinding corn
chafing of stone on pumice stone,
it was tortillas and chile
with oregano.

A radio warms up to
"Operación de Limpieza'"
though later strangely silent.

A padre at the river bank
sees a thick canopy of buzzards,
May 14, 1980.

The motive was clear.

Bullets fell in fistfuls,
their skin black,
their eyes melted like fat.

Beyond Las Aradas
fishermen retrieved their ghastly nets.

Long days in the bush.
An arc of fifteen bullets
from her thigh to the small of her back.

Convivial, highly democratic, soldiers
toast victory with blood and oregano,
the water full of blood.

Tío Angel with his mouth wide open
washing over with water
that smelled of garlic or rum.

II.

Outside Saltillo she braided her hair
and a rivulet ran back to the source
of Río Martín.

Butterflies were with us
braiding the air around our heads.

And when we spoke
we talked of our lives since the Sierra
grainy details of juniper in ferreous canyons
burros loaded with cilantro and pulque.

Something I remembered:
They picked him up very gently
and carried him away.

The nakedness of women is the work of God.
The skin between her breasts oily first
dusted with talc, the darkness of her sex
ganglia and scent, my voice
at night deeper broken susurando.

In bed in England dreaming
beautiful wars of infamous music
in the rocks of Northern Mexico.

But do not read to me.
At this tilt, any words will seem sibilant,
profound, intractable. The words
Beauty Freedom Remorse
are Persian, impossible, beyond us all.

When the sun comes out
road signs burn in tropic light
no forgiveness amidst limestone
rivers and palm.

Somotillo

Tossed out of bed in an earthquake dream,
where rustling of leaves was gusting smoke
from the volcano at Masaya, or was artillery
echoing at dawn from the far side of the lake.

Across a tree-shaded concrete patio, the parrot
sauntered in the gait of a Hollywood cowboy
mimicking last night's monologue in an accent
that reminded us of Cantinflas in English.

"Satán weel not ween! Weel no ween!"
the bird shrilled, hoarse from his hours
of chatter in that otherwise happy place.
We recalled seeing the empire in the distance:

how under clouds, its skyscrapers and towers
had faded into temples, ziggurats, pyramids,
and giant stelae. How lights blinking in haze,
became only stars, mirrors, candles in salt air.

When a hush fell, it brought rumblings of the
beginning of disaster, and the parade was set
to commence. While the leaves stirred like flames
costumed crowds stood quietly, waiting for alarms.

The widows at the village well were spellbound,
staring at the water where the sun's reflection
was dissolving into millions of pulsing atoms,
helping them forget their burdens of mourning.
They saw no measure was possible, to say if the
rites of sin and penance were ever sufficient.

It was to be the first day in a new dream's calendar,
every moment become weightless as the breath of birds.

Abuelos

They stroll like cloistered nuns in the square at Sabinas
stopping to hand roll smokes beneath the avocado trees.
Priests and prostitutes shiver just to see them there.

But to forget grandfathers, I'll write "I never knew mine"
and neither did my parents, or hardly, before they died.
When our histories assume only what we'd have them be
my own has no grandfathers, no claw mustaches, no silk cravat.
Their names I dispute as legends, their careers on the land.

We became American on premiums of Prudential Life
insurance policies and clever trade in the new language.
There was a world of complicated engines and shrill radios
when scarce money drew Mexicans to foundries, smelting iron
stoop-backed, or to cantaloupe fields, bathing in ditches.
The vigor of commerce might've touched them, in Spaniard blood
upright over ledgers on the roll-top desk. In Cotulla's red dust
industry and English mixed in the reek of ceniza and tar.

They meant to leave us nothing, working all their lives
so we should forget them and how they came away
from an ancient world of burro carts and adobe Madonnas.

There is something of smells to their title in the old language
and to sniff at the knees of their britches was maybe tobacco,
resin of chrysanthemum leaves or camphor, their hands
maybe, of loam and beer. What separates us is more than time
or place. My world is unreal, like a film about memory or time
while they planted ferns in underground gardens of the grocer padrón.

I forget them completely in a foreign country. I forget
how the first died by water, the other beneath linen
in underwear, a child wiping silver froth from his lips.

I reckon them only as stories we continue
to pass on, pieces of a lost world with endless carnivals
of death and dark men. And we are all forgetting
what we are meant to forget, whether faces or letters,
or a hillside in morning darkness where a funeral train
passed once, lit with candles, lumbering south to Laredo.

La Ruta

That road ran farther back
than maps or memory allowed.
Once, it was the road where all roads began
shadowing the Gulf coast
with palm, banana, bougainvillea,
then slowly climbing toward the Sierra,
past jacalas decked with tamarind,
honey and vanilla.

Pearl-colored smoke came up
from the burning fields
in plumes that spun every gust
into spirals, churning and dissolving
into the jungle's amber light.
The worksongs of the farmers
glittered with tentacles of fire.

When no road can return us
to its beginning, that place has gone
to where stars, in daytime,
hide their light.

Muñeca de San Ángel

Working the squeezebox behind the wheel
watching a western in his small room in Coatepec
she was partly of that world, tropical and ancient
and her laughter was all tamarind and mischief.

(Blood clotted with mixiote and chile)

From a fatherless clan, left to the streets, taken in
by pirates, petty thieves, slick-haired vatos
who separate decent folk from their money.

Hawking tamales by the ruins
where all I can offer her is the way back
how to find the centripetal center
past the turning vastness
of avenidas, plazas, pereféricos.
A woman whose breath was the pure ether
of another woman's whole chemistry.

Walk a lament without words.
Let it rotate slowly through the four houses
of blood, breath, bone and song.

Waking to bugles when la guardia came out
 to raise the colors, and the streets still full of haze.

The viejo of ninety years, pariente
in denim jacket, turning over dirt
on his third wife's grave, sinking from heavy rains.

He dreamed with us, praying all along:
Machete. Vanilla. Honey and ash.
Totonac. Olmec. Mexica. Chichimeca.

Tzompantepec. Xicochimalco. Ixhuacan.
Ayahualulco. Jalapa. Zempoala. Cholula.

Rotating, turning slowly, toward the next eclipse.

At the Hill of Old Boots

Little Fidéncio swung the bull-roarer,
and it sang in wide arcs, con la voz de dios,
basso profundo, swift and thunderous,
floating on the treetops in a whorl
toward a silvery dusk horizon.

There was no chile pequín this year.
No wild mountain oregano.
Frozen in May, the peach trees
were blooming in October,
and the mariposas monarcas,
didn't migrate south through the serranía,
as they had since creation time.

"Such are these days," my Uncle said.
"You have been away a very long time."

Looking at old photographs from Oaxaca,
"Grandfather was puro Indio," he said,
"Mixteco o Zapoteco." Out of that time,
he was poised now in an everlasting stare,
moreno, dressed like a charro on a horse,
his saddle filigreed in bright maguey thread.

Many years before, my cousin and I
had fed flies and crickets to the ranch spiders,
until they were too fat to spin their webs.
Remembering this, years later,
I left my boots behind, like a penance.

This morning, I put them on again.

Then we rode out the trail to El Milagro,
and el tío said,
"These hills never change in a thousand years."

Then I looked across the rolling summits,
softened ages ago in the briny velvet wash
of an ancient receding sea, and the dawn star
was still shining, flickering its perpetual light.

The Memory Prayer

I learned to breathe this way
when I left that body made of ashes,
river water, copal and huisache flowers.

When my breath was South
it was a feather as big as a palm frond.
The infinite miles were numbered in stars
and the earth was lit from inside.

My eyes were mirrors, my heart was wind.
The ground pulled my songs like a magnet.

The bananas were so ripe they spread like butter
when they first brought guns into the garden.

Our legacy is papaya, is frijol,
is sangria by the gallons.

Helix inside of helix, the color of blood.
Dead uncles. Lost friends. Forgotten amantes.

For five hundred years of impossible weather,
this lightning has smelled like night,
weaving its net of forgetting across these lands.

Peregrinos

Our feet swoop and trudge in immaculate deep alluvial sand,
pedaling stars and galaxies, talking in spikes and plumes
through currents of hoarse wind as colorless as lily petal tea.

The map shows this desert one thousand miles wide.

I will carry the monkey rattle.
I will protect the painted shards.
I will chant the ancestors' names.
I will cast their jade again.

For every chile there is a star, and for every star, a breath
is drawn far into the north, far past desert and sierra.

Someone stitches the fan belt with whisker-thin fencing wire.
The chorizo cures as hard as leather, fideos are cooked in fennel.
Before we sleep, I will wash your neck, you will bathe my feet.
We eat dates and tell stories, knowing that we are taking the long way.

La Diosa de Maguey

The huisaches were alive with monarchs
and chapote bushes bristled with galaxies of ants.
Thorny garrabatos, like the claws of a cat,
trailed spiderwebs, as banners in her honor.

In this desert flamenco heaven, I wondered
if the skin of her neck tasted of leche quemada,
if her breath had the fragrance of flowery yolixpi.

But she sat alone, draped in a fiery serape,
singing to tecolotes as they floated past her on the hilltop.

"Es la sirena de la sierra," the old vaquero called her.
"Do not dance with that demonia colorada!"

She made the sky turn the color of maguey,
a phosphorus greenish grey, and in that baptismal light,
her flesh glowed with a thousand ghostly thorns.

I would set myself before her, if she allows me
avoiding her eyes behind the undulating veils,
and leave behind my offerings:
exquisite sierra honey, an apple dipped in chile,
a green and pink grasshopper, encased in fresh beeswax.

Rancho Sandía

We planted watermelons in shallow sand
as pale as shells, hoping the vines
would grow to the south and away from
a stand of blooming cactus at the rusty
windmill's base. But then leathery leaves

sprouted, curling on their stalks,
and copperheads and horned toads
found shade there, nestling their scaly
bellies into the patch's furrows,
still damp from the morning drizzle.

"We cannot argue with the animals,"
my father said, staring. "It's good they go
where they want." Anywhere but with my *sandía*,
I thought. And when we roasted goat,
basting it with lime juice, cumin,

and cilantro, uncles would stand
over those melons telling how
blackbirds waited for hot days
to pierce the fuzzy husks with their beaks,
sucking the fruits dry, one by one.

Maybe a scarecrow could save them,
maybe a mean dog, or maybe we could
just buy a watermelon on the way back to town,
they said, laughing into the thin necks
of their bottles of beer.

While back in the city, Mexicans
gathered nightly by picnic benches
under a tent on Fredericksburg Road,

eating salted watermelon
in sickle-shaped slices,
spitting seeds into the moonlight.

Daykeeping

Shall we drive on, whatever may come
ignoring the rumors echoing through Tuxtla?
The army battalions are poised for ambush
insurgent Maya waiting to pounce after them.
That the road to San Cristobal is closed.
That there is not a godly soul on that road tonight.

They were right; only fog and moonlight.

Ghostly radio whisper of sitar and chant in the hills
as we drove our computers, gems and astrolabe
into far precincts of a revolution from the ancients.

They stood in the stone road, shoulder to shoulder
woven huipiles and ponchos, sandals, barefoot.

To slow our way or block it altogether
los militantes used tree trunks, the ejército
great boulders and stones. I told the jóven
if we should not reach Ocosingo tonight
the life of this unborn child is on your head
and the Virgencita have mercy on you.
But you would not want to be haunted
by that for the rest of your life, would you?

Palenque bats escorted us the rest of the way.

Pearl light of Arcturus danced in lily spirals
across the courtyard, shimmer of Pollux
upon the glass tabletop. There, and then not.
As bombs fell like bougainvillea firecrackers
across the hills, we drew our separate maps
puzzling the unnumbered quanta of Mexico
that first brought us into this exploding world.

Chiapas Sonnets

I.

At the church in Chamula, in those first days
of the New Year's War, prayers still gushed
from the lips of old Mayan men and women,
kneeling on a floor, strewn with statues and pine needles.
Four elders kept their unbroken watch in shadows
while time passed as slowly as thick wax dripping
at the feet of their elaborate, adorned shrines.
The prayers they made were to gods and saints
for easy births, grace in battle, or for the recently dead.
Maybe San Juan was a Zapatista, or maybe a Priista
but the compromisos of living and dying
had never been interrupted by any war.
The incense-filled air made a sacrament of Pepsi
as we wandered through, wrapped in our secret awe.

II.

Someone left tacos de nopalitos at our doorstep,
wrapped in newspaper, like a Christmas present.
That morning we awoke and climbed the roof to see
Army helicopters dropping bombs on Rancho Nuevo,
and for the rest of the day, the streets were scattered
with scarlet petals of San Cristobal's bougainvillea.
Not long ago, los Indios couldn't use the sidewalks.
Making war against them now, the old bishop said,
"is like a Mexican killing their own Mother."
An astrologer said, "This is the birth of a new Mexico."
And that night, as we embraced in a magenta kirilian glow,
musicians and singers of Las Posadas passed by outside,
so we joined them, behind the violins and the trumpets
in those callejones full of peregrinos and refugees.

Saving Light

Fireflies know this better than the rest of us:
Only so much light in this universe.
Out of a great flaring forth into formless dark,
they count only so many stars to be lit, so many novas
pinwheel nebulae, eclipses of the moon.

A young girl sees them flicker for the first time
in a glen by the reservoir. The fireflies ask her:
"What will remain of these lime glow trails
when pearly agate ice covers the world again?"
In a glint, their glimmer incandesces matte night air
then floats out of time between the blades of grass.

Because it is a cyclical story, after all, because
the chambers of a shell spiral precisely around an axis
she will see this light again, moving out toward the horizon.

The light bulb in the bodega dims at midnight.
Most of the inevitable starlight will never be seen.
Years later, she blows out a candle at dawn
in a world of light, dimming now by infinite scintillas.

New Sun

In a scintilla of Coahuila sunlight,
so amber at the end of the day
it becomes a kiss that lasts an hour,
I want to fall, silent and fierce

like a meteor made of lunar ice,
an arrow point of flame, careening
without flesh, musculature or bone,
lighting on the thorn of a flowering cactus.

When these hills were covered in salt water
salamanders the color of Tlaxcala jade
dreamed such a light would someday come,
and their dreaming made it happen.

When coyotes first spilled the blood of rabbits
and that day ended a deeper red than ever before,
the ancestors commemorated that time
as the first day of our new sun.

Through Coahuila sky, I fall for centuries
twirling in whirlwinds of butterflies and feathers.
The stars rise the color of pomegranate seeds
and stones rumble all along the infinite sierra.

A Legend

When there were too few of them to sing the old songs
then silence became their song.
Their pockets were full of eucalyptus leaves
and their voices cracked from liquor, smoke and laughing
when silence became their song.
They thought that god might be sad, missing the old songs
and they wondered if they could still dream
when silence became their song.
So they gathered in the quiet, and they sang a silent dream
of the hand of god, emerging from a golden hoop in the sky
that left all of creation in its wake
when silence became their song.

Winter Menu

We ate mushrooms four times a week,
watching capillaries of snow swell and glisten
along dark ridges of the far mountain.

"It feels like minus one," she said.
"It feels just below zero."

The harder the winter, the fiercer the flower.
That will come soon, won't it? You quietly wonder
if the season will change again ever, the implausible
jade blooming, the numberless shoots and sprigs.

In omelets, in sauces, soups and stir-fry:
porcini, crimini, shitake, oyster, and chanterelle.
Every arc against the bow was a swift crescent.
Every tone fit inevitably into its measure.

We awaited the flood that would wash away
that world encumbered by ice. We lit the stove
and warmed the pan with cloves and olive oil.

Untitled

If you live in a place where nothing happens,
soldiers are lurking somewhere nearby,
smoking, gargling whisky, keeping the peace.

When planted thick, a garden bakes inside its hedges.

If rain water percolates through soggy turf there,
that is experience, in the hearing of it.

Almost a world without experiences
save those things which persist in falling:
massive trucks rattling back to the dairy
and every hour a train through the rail yard.

Your acts are reproduced as dumb machines.

One by one, we patented testimonies on tea
or terrorism, as if to confirm that knowledge
is impossible unless there's a world first.

And yet, no knowledge is necessary in any world.

Whether you like it or not, life is always
about something, absent from the inside,
in the way papery husks of strong garlic
reveal the skeletons of the missing cloves.

Deep Field

I.

We unscroll bolts of damask linen, measuring every incongruous hem
with an Osage arrow, a Hawawir sword, any ruins left lying around the place.
With open palm and fiery heart, bring in our whisperer of suras,
crescent halo, penumbrae of a thousand shimmering kites.
Let words rise like ether of gardenia, bringing love, forgetting and adrenaline.

II.

Roll back the sky now. Roll it back on a scroll
stapled with cactus spines, tightened around the polestar
every swath dotted with squash flowers and pine tar,
all our parole glistening in a wash of opal sea foam.
That's how far back we had to go to find the way
again, that's where we left all the counted stones
where blood that runs as clear as honeysuckle sap
mingled with our breath, night air, turning burgundy
forever. "It was a poignant century," said the old priest
"a century when we thought we were doing good,
when we were really doing very bad." The sky
remembers everything, each pulse of fire, flame tracks
of the first songs, the first contrition of the void
giving forth, inexhaustible, leavening the quiet.
When we hear the song again, it's an old radio show
scratchy as if it had traveled across time
in a meteor of smoky quartz. When we embrace
an open canyon yawns beneath us, languid cool air
swirling, twirling us westward into oldest night.

Prodigals

The plains were dotted with pearly ocotillo flowers.
It was in those days we found our way, skies already
had churned for weeks, magma surging deep below
until it burst the earth's fittings and lit up the lands
that had long since cooled from the heat of first fire.

And they're ringing the oldest bells again tonight
shaking all our bones to the sweetest part of the marrow.
Oldest bells cast of bronze, unalloyed silver and platinum
in a tower that once reached into the thinnest clouds.
The bells, now deep underwater, ring and ring for us.

We are in the mustang plains again tonight.
Once, we were left behind here, blown like seeds
thrown far from the stands of dry ocotillo stalks.
We had not known that we had survived, how serenatas
awaited us and uncounted stars would shine once more.

No lesson can suffice to learn those songs we knew.
When your scent surrounds me, it is a desert scarf
damask and gold, veiling me from unforgiving light.
I say to you we could travel by night, we could
make our way by the brightest star's beacons.

Az´ul is everywhere. Azul, pardo, pink flames
a new river flowing, made of the fiery waves
we sail our little brigantina upon, grasping the tiller
steering on, and the sails are stretched tight
with gusts sent from our first, long-forgotten home.

Late Dispatch

Tractor teeth braided sandy Russian mud
churning tracks through the forest of engines.
They used rusting rockets to slop pigs,
dropped Sherman tanks into the Gulf
so they might become webs of glowing coral
future harbor for snapper, reds, mahi mahi.
Didn't you receive that end-of-the-year letter?
Paper like starched vellum, every dendrite
of antique brown ink a filigree of a filigree.
Something strange and wonderful was planned.
Did these tidings arrive before you set out?
Dropping tethers from the river's grassy bank
into the great stream of beckoning souls.
That story got to me, in case you were wondering
a whisper to me in the heart of a blue norther.
And did you know how short our spell of peace
would last before we'd be counting the light
like precious beans to last the long dark?

Landfall

I did not mean to be born once more.
Amber light gathered over turquoise water
as it never would ever again. Rain for days
washed our city clean, the color of limestone.

Then we cast off, armed only with portolani
in an ark made of mesquite, tracing coastlines
with nowhere in sight to land for weeks.
It was such a land as had never been dreamed
fiery mountains, alabaster sand, swaying palms
as if we might never drop anchor anywhere.

We wondered if we could ever find the way home.
But she said it was "as if we were always here"
wrapped in magenta sails, we tumbled seaward
laughing into bodies that seemed weightless
divested of everything that was ever forlorn
sadness of heartbreak, exile, war, the end of time.

I did not mean to breathe in such delight
ojos de aurora verde, pelo rojo, piel vanilla.
I had not suspected her essential alma could be
hidden away under the deep for centuries or more.

So I was born into this body when lightning
struck the cerulean waters of a forgotten gulf.
I never imagined walking out of saltwater onto land
again, my lungs filling at once with sweet, first air.

About the Author

John Phillip Santos recently returned to his hometown of San Antonio, Texas, after twenty-one years in New York. He was (and remains) a freelance filmmaker, producer, journalist and writer whose work focuses on issues of media, culture and ethnic identity. His articles have appeared in the *Los Angeles Times* and the *New York Times,* among numerous other publications. A former executive producer and director of new program development for Thirteen/WNET, Santos also produced over 40 documentaries for CBS and PBS, two of them nominated for Emmy Awards. In 1997, Santos joined the Ford Foundation as an officer in the Media, Arts and Culture Program, where he handled the Media Projects Fund and worked with new media technologies, especially as they pertain to developing countries.

Santos was the first Mexican-American Rhodes scholar to study at Oxford. He holds degrees in English Literature and Language from Oxford University and in Philosophy and Literature from the University of Notre Dame. He is a recipient of the Academy of American Poets' Prize at Notre Dame and the Oxford Prize for fiction. Santos is currently a Visiting Fellow at the Watson Institute for International Studies at Brown University.

Santos' 1999 family memoir, *Places Left Unfinished at the Time of Creation* (Viking / Penguin) was a finalist for the National Book Award. In 2006 it was selected for the "One Book, One City" reading program in San Antonio. *Places Left Unfinished at the Time of Creation* is a beautifully crafted work – a haunting prose poem to a city, a region, and a people, interwoven with Mexican mythology, Chicano folk tales, family stories, and dreams.

Colophon

This edition of *Songs Older Than Any Know Singer* by John Phillip Santos has been printed on 70 pound non-acidic paper containing fifty percent recycled fiber. The text has been set in Adobe Caslon Type; poem titles in Cochin Type, book and section titles in Whiffy Type. The first 25 signature sets to be pulled from the press have been numbered and signed by the author. All Wings Press books are designed by Bryce Milligan.

Wings Press was founded in 1975 by Joanie Whitebird and Joseph F. Lomax, both deceased, as "an informal association of artists and cultural mythologists dedicated to the preservation of the literature of the nation of Texas." The publisher/editor since 1995, Bryce Milligan is honored to carry on and expand that mission to include the finest in American writing, without commercial considerations clouding the choice to publish or not to publish. We know well that writing is a transformational art form capable of changing the world, primarily by allowing us to glimpse something of each other's souls. Good writing is innovative, insightful, and interesting. But most of all it is honest. In a similar spirit, Wings Press is committed to treating the planet itself as a partner. Thus we use as much recycled material as possible, from the paper on which the books are printed to the boxes in which they are shipped.

Wings Press titles are distributed to the trade by
The Independent Publishers Group • www.ipgbook.com